Lincolnshire Artists

One Hundred Years 1906 - 2006

Edward Mayor

An illustrated history of the Lincolnshire Artists' Society originally known as the Lincolnshire Drawing Club

Published in 2006 by the Lincolnshire Artists' Society.

ISBN 0-9552939-0-1

Cover illustration: Peter Williams, Passage from The Nelson Mass: 'Et Incarnatus'.
Title page illustration: 'LAS 1906-2006' Watercolour by Ken Lee.

Book compiled by Max Marschner, David Morris and David Paton.

Designed and printed by Ruddocks Design & Print, Great Northern Terrace, Lincoln.

British Cataloguing-in-Publication Data
A catalogue record for this book is obtainable from the British Library.

Acknowledgements

The writing of this first history of the Lincolnshire Artists' Society 1906-2006 was made possible with the generous assistance of the Usher Gallery Trust.

The Society's President Peter Moss and current Chairman Carol Butler, provided archival material and introduced me to many contributors. I am deeply grateful for their help and support.

Max Marschner, David Morris and David Paton undertook the design and choice of illustrations and I am grateful for their expertise and good humour.

Andrea Martin, Jeremy Webster and the staff of the Usher Gallery and The Collection have generously enabled me to work from the yearbooks and have shared their visual database, taking an enthusiastic interest in the project.

Particular thanks must go to the Usher Gallery, The Collection, and Lincolnshire County Council for making numerous pictures and objects from their collections available for reproduction. Also to North East Lincolnshire Museums for permission to reproduce 'Alexandra Dock' by Herbert Rollett.

The staff of the Central Lincoln Library, the Lincolnshire Archives and the Lincolnshire Echo have been very helpful, and thanks must also be given to Aleisha Scott for her Echo article which began the project. The Lincolnshire Echo has kindly given permission for reproduction of the photograph of members of the selection committee at work in the Usher Gallery in 1948.

The following have given generously of their time and memories: Nancy and Gordon Baldwin, Shelia Bartl, Noel Black, Mavis Brannan, Christopher Brighton, Cilla Chapman, Laraine Cooper, Magie Dean, Nick Ellerby, Mary Fitzpayne, Richard Hatfield, Jenny Hammerton, David Hollinshead, Jane Kennedy, Janice Kok, Marie and Ken Lee, Dr John Lord, Max Marschner, Frank Marston, David Morris, David Paton, Keith Roper, Gillian Ross-Kelsey, Jeannie Rowan, Allen Smith, Charles Speed, Fenella Stoner, Marjorie, John, Tim and Robin Wheeldon, Dr Peter Williams, Alison Wilson, Geoffrey Wilson and Richard Wood.

My partner Jonathan Perks typed the text onto disc and his help and advice have been invaluable.

My grateful thanks go to everyone mentioned above.

On a sadder note, Peter Williams the distinguished art educationalist and artist, died only days after sending me his foreword. May his memory, cherished by the Society and by many in Lincoln, find an expression in these pages and glow from our cover, which was specially chosen in tribute.

Edward R Mayor. February '06

Contents

Foreword - A Society for Artists, Run by Artists

The urge to record and communicate the sheer enjoyment of visual experience lies deep in human nature and has taken a multitude of forms over many centuries. This remarkable story of Lincolnshire's own Artists' Society provides a wonderful insight into the determination, dedication and effort, as well as the passion and pitfalls generated when creative talents come together. If we peek between the lines of this meticulous study we can join committee members in their frustrations and share in their successes, back them in their struggle against parochialism, flinch at their petty jealousies and sympathise with the general membership's bewilderment as policies come and go. More positively, however, we can stand back and admire the enormous influence of the Society over the last 100 years as a generator of creative activity in the visual arts across this large county.

The significance of such effort should not be underestimated, for, as well as facilitating the social contact and the exchange of ideas so fundamental to artistic work, the Society, from an early date, opened its doors to any person wishing to try their hand and provided a stimulus for improvement. In so doing it not only brought new sources of pleasure and self-knowledge to many hundreds of practitioners but also enabled them to experience at first hand the challenge and rewards of creative pursuits. Ironically, this enlightened policy also laid the foundations for later conflict and uncertainty.

From a small, tightly knit base of the leisured classes and clergy in 1906, the Society quickly opened out to include a significant proportion of mature professional artists largely generated by the Lincoln School of Art (opened in 1863). This process, however, laid the ground for confrontation between them and the substantial 'amateur' membership. The seeds of discontent are clear from a very early date, but a visiting critic's adverse comments on the absence of innovative work in the 50's appears to have played a pivotal role in the growing demand for change. In the 60's resistance grew to the acceptance of 'Sunday painters' within the Society. The 70's produced a policy of actively recruiting professional practitioners. In the 80's the Usher Gallery forcibly expressed concern about inconsistent quality. While past achievements were fully acknowledged, a fundamental shift in purpose and objectives became inevitable.

In 1993 it came. The balance altered and the focus changed. The increasingly professional approach of members set new targets and standards. Fortunately, however, these also did not long remain unchallenged. Now controversy surfaces around such issues as craft-based v conceptual, handmade v new technology, traditional v contemporary. These are some of the debates that continue to give vigour and muscle to progressive artists and craft people and they augur well for the future.

In summary, Edward Mayor's valuable and highly readable book draws together in an unusual way the innermost workings of a dynamic and highly successful Society, revealing highs and lows of 100 years of artistic endeavour as expressed through the personalities and issues of each period. Here is a Society for artists run by artists, and long may it be so!

Peter Williams – October 2005

Introduction - Art in a Vast County

Lincolnshire, the second largest county in England, has been famously depicted by JMW Turner, Thomas Girtin and Peter de Wint, and many less famous artists. De Wint (1784 – 1849) captured the majesty of Lincoln's great cathedral from almost every angle. A native of Stone in Staffordshire, he eventually came to Lincoln, married Harriet Hilton, the sister of his close friend William Hilton, the history painter, and lived in the uphill area of the city for several years.

Visible from thirty or even forty miles in some directions, Lincoln Cathedral has been the inevitable Lincolnshire motif, as powerful as the Mont St. Victoire in the work of Paul Cezanne. The county's fenlands, wolds, shoreline and churches have also offered rich subject-matter to many artists, some of whom joined the Lincolnshire Artists' Society, but Lincoln Cathedral continued to be a major source of inspiration, and Lincoln itself was the inevitable headquarters for the county's leading art society, especially since 1927 when the Usher Gallery was opened by Edward, Prince of Wales.

The Lincolnshire Artists' Society did not spring fully formed from unprepared ground. Far from being the cultural backwater many imagine, Lincoln had an art school with links to Antwerp and Paris. The Lincoln public were used to seeing art, ever since the first exhibition of work by students of the School of Art and Design, held in the winter of 1864. Opened in 1863 as a private venture by Canon John Somerville Gibney, who hired a room in the Old Corn Exchange, the School moved to the top of a building in Silver Street, to a new room specially added and designed by Lincoln architect Michael Drury, in October 1864. In 1886 the School moved to new premises on Monks Road designed by London architect D. Sedger, which from the start was a School of Science and Art. From 1877 the headmaster of the Art School was Alfred G. Webster, who would play an important part in the early days of the Society.

Webster developed an important link with the Royal Academy of Antwerp which was shared only with Birmingham School of Art. It was encouraged by Charles Verlat, admired teacher and Anglophile, who taught at Antwerp between 1878 and 1885. Several prominent members of the Lincolnshire Artists' Society, such as Frank Bramley, William Logsdail, Fred Hall and George Boden, were trained first at the Lincoln School of Art, then at Antwerp. Another Lincoln born and trained artist, William T. Warrener, actually moved to Paris and showed his work at the Paris Salon. He became a member of Toulouse-Lautrec's circle and his image appears in Lautrec's 'The Englishman at the Moulin Rouge'. Lautrec caught perfectly the appearance of a man later described as 'an immaculate gentleman with a monocle'. He returned to Lincoln in 1904, and became the Society's first Chairman.

Two of Lincoln's foremost industrialists, Alfred Shuttleworth and Joseph Ruston, had superb art collections featuring works by Sir Edward Burne-Jones and many Royal Academicians, Shuttleworth's home being on Lincoln's Eastgate and Ruston's being further east at Monks Manor. The Society would be born in Monks Manor and eventually hold most of its meetings at Shuttleworth's Eastgate Court, which by the 1920's was an hotel.

Facing Eastgate Court, on Cathedral Green, was the powerful statue of Alfred Lord Tennyson with his wolfhound Karenina, designed by George Frederick Watts, who did not live to witness its unveiling by the Countess Brownlow in 1905. Many of the original members of the Society, or the Lincolnshire Drawing Club as it was called, at first, must have been present at that event, for many of them lived and worked around the Cathedral.

Such was the fertile ground in which a Society of Artists, similar to several already formed around England, could flourish. Moreover, John Ruskin the foremost writer on art in Victorian England, had remarked in a letter to the Page family of Lincoln that its cathedral was 'out and out the most precious piece of architecture we possess' and 'worth two of any of the others'. This assessment, delivered in a speech when a member of the Page family became Mayor of Lincoln, must have resonated amongst the cultured community there.

The moment had arrived.

The Lincolnshire Drawing Club

William Warrener, *Leonline*

"Sketching is such a nice occupation for a young lady, as they used to say in those days" (Gwen Raverat, 'Period Piece')

On June 2nd 1906, Miss Elsie Ruston, a daughter of the Lincoln Industrialist and art-collector Joseph Ruston, held a meeting at her family home, Monks Manor, which would result in a long term reinvigoration of the artistic life of Lincolnshire. She proposed the formation of the Lincolnshire Drawing Club, in which pictures exhibited annually, by an amateur membership, would be criticised by someone of standing in the art world. Miss Ruston could scarcely have imagined that the artistic endeavours of herself and a wide circle of friends would, within six years, lead to considerable interest from the local press and public, and a change of name to the Lincolnshire Artists' Society, which it has been called ever since. She would have been even more surprised that many of the top names in British art would visit Lincoln as a direct result of the high quality of the exhibitions.

It was another of Joseph Ruston's daughters, Ethel (Mrs. Walter Heape) who would inspire Elsie to form the Lincolnshire Drawing Club. Ethel was already connected with the Cambridge Drawing Society, founded in 1882 by Lady Sandys, the wife of the Public Orator. The Society did not hold exhibitions, but met regularly in drawing rooms for practical sessions and talks. Gwen Raverat, the distinguished illustrator and an eventual president of the Society, recalled in her book 'Period Piece', how in her youth, a Miss Mary Greene would hold inspirational art classes and give art-history lectures to young ladies. Then, in the same year as the Lincoln Club was founded, the Cambridge Society decided it, too, would exhibit and invite guest critics, attracting artists of the calibre of Sickert and Henry Tonks.

The Rustons and their circle are to be commended for their seriousness of purpose in engaging from the outset the services of prominent art educationalists, critics or artists. The first, appropriately, was Alfred G. Webster, headmaster of the Lincoln School of Art. Printed leaflets were issued featuring his name as the first critic along with a few simple rules for entering work for the exhibition, but the all-female management committee of four with their honorary secretary Miss Elsie Ruston had not thought to devise any aims or objectives. They fixed the subscription at three shillings annually and informed members that an Annual General Meeting would be held after each exhibition. And they decided to award Mr.

William Warrener, *Quadrille I*

Webster the sum of two guineas for his criticisms, a duty later described by the press as 'decidedly delicate'! Members could exhibit up to five pictures.

Mrs. R. Mason, a founder member and honorary secretary after Miss Ruston, recalled in 1956 that 'our first exhibition was held in two loose boxes at Monks Manor.' Joseph Ruston had given his permission for part of his stables to be used, and on Friday and Saturday the 9th and 10th November 1906, the exhibition was open for members and guests, between 2pm and 6pm. Mr. Webster's criticisms were given at 10.45am on the Friday, to interested members only. And, in a pattern which would repeat itself for many years, the Annual

William Warrener, *Garden Pathway*

Miss Iris Reeve's 'Negroes, Nomads and Dust' at 14 guineas. Lady Cholmeley showed three paintings of Norway, and Elsie Ruston, clearly benefiting from a recent visit to Egypt, showed 'Theban Hills at Sunrise'.

It was not clear how many of the exhibits were drawings but the rules stated that 'drawings and paintings' should be framed and labelled. There were also pastel studies.

1907

Of the 49 founder members, only 4 were male. They were a Mr. C. Brook of Pottergate, Lincoln, the Rev. Canon Harvey of Navenby, Major-General Richardson of Spilsby, and William Thomas Warrener of St. Margaret's Lodge, Lincoln. Warrener, 1861-1934 was a Lincoln-born and trained artist of repute who enjoyed some success in France and had been depicted by Toulouse-Lautrec as the 'Englishman at the Moulin Rouge'. In 1904 he was obliged to give up his artistic career and return to Lincoln to run the family coal business after his brother had died, but he obviously relished his membership of the Drawing Club and in 1907 was proposing to the AGM that 'Lincolnshire Professionals' should be asked to join, and send pictures to the exhibitions. Elsie Ruston proposed that of five works that might be submitted by each member, only 3 should be labelled 'for criticism'. Perhaps George Clausen, RA, had found that commenting on every one of the 188 exhibits in the 1907 exhibition was an exhausting task. He was probably invited on Webster's recommendation, since the two men were brothers-in-law, and Clausen was a distinguished painter of figures working in the landscape, bringing, with Warrener, a bright post Impressionist palette to Lincoln. While there is no record of the reaction to Webster's criticisms, the 1907 AGM records that 'Unanimous and hearty votes of thanks were accorded to Mr. Clausen for coming to criticise the drawings'. And Clausen was awarded 3 guineas more than Webster. 12 pictures were sold, an increase of 5 over the previous year.

General Meeting followed the exhibition. In 1906 this was held at Monks Manor on November the 19th. Out of the 142 exhibits, seven pictures were sold, but only 55 were priced in the catalogue.

Lincolnshire and foreign travel featured prominently in the subject matter on view in 1906. Canon Harvey offered four Venetian subjects in what would be his first and last exhibition before his death in 1907. Miss Denny of Minster Yard portrayed the Cantilupe Chantry, Langworth Gate, and James Street, all Lincoln subjects. Miss Isobel Hutton showed 'September Morning, Steep Hill' and asked six guineas for it, but more expensive was

Harold Coop, *Bakewell, Derbyshire*

1908

The loose-boxes were succeeded by three 'temporary salons', erected in the grounds of Monks Manor, for the 1903 exhibition. The Lincolnshire Echo described the Drawing Club as 'this private society', and the Lincolnshire Gazette joined with the Echo in bemoaning the fact that until then the Club had 'not chosen to come very prominently before the public eye'. This did not mean that it had decided to allow the public to see the exhibition, for that would have to wait until 1909, but at least the Press were now involved, and they reacted very favourably, rejoicing that at last they were allowed to tell the public what a 'delightful gallery of pencil and brush sketches' was 'arranged in its midst.' The critic was Mr. Morley Fletcher, Director of the Edinburgh College of Art, who gave members 'an interesting review of their work.' At the AGM, the Misses St. Leger and Matthew proposed that he be asked back in 1909, while the Misses Swan and Bergne-Coupland proposed that the exhibition should be open to the public at the charge of 6d including catalogue, with schoolchildren at half-price.

William Logsdail, *An Early Victorian*

Frank Bramley ARA, another Lincoln trained artist from Sibsey near Boston, had been invited to exhibit alongside the members, and he was described in the Press as the 'star turn'. Other 'star turns' invited by Warrener included Lincoln-trained William Logsdail, Fred Hall, and George Carline RBA, the brother of a Lincoln doctor, who would all feature in 1909.

1909 A Little Local Difficulty

The last exhibition to be held at Monks Manor was also the first to admit the public. Joseph Ruston decided to exhibit his study of 'Vesuvius from Pompeii', while Elsie showed subjects from Mexico, which 'justifiably attracted a good deal of attention'. She was, however, no longer the Club's Honorary Secretary. In a most unusual development, the founder had resigned.

On Friday July 9th, an Extra General Meeting was held at Monks Manor with Warrener in the chair. Elsie was present, and announced her resignation 'through unforeseen circumstances'. The minutes record that 'a vote of censure was passed on the retiring Hon. Sec.' A few moments later, Mrs. Mason was elected in Elsie's place. Perhaps the speed of Elsie's betrothal and marriage to Michael Thomas Lloyd Apjohn had been responsible for this upset, but it would explain her Mexican pictures of Pueblo dwellings and 'broncos', for her new address was Bar Diamond Ranch, Pecos, New Mexico.

Ample press notices praised Warrener, Logsdail, Isobel Hutton and the Misses Richardson whose 'extremely clever watercolours of Cornwall and Gibraltar' were 'most habile'. It seems that Morley Fletcher had been unable to return and in his place came Archibald Hartrick, of the New English Art Club and the Royal Watercolour Society. There is no record of his reception, but he criticised the Exhibition on Thursday October 21st. 178 pictures were exhibited but only 7 were sold. Membership had also fallen to 70.

1910

The 1910 Exhibition saw Warrener as the critic as well as the Chairman, standing in for an unnamed critic of his choice, who was clearly unable to come. The Lincolnshire Gazette said that 'he expressed freely his opinion, praising here (and stating why), advising there and including many helpful hints in a running commentary that was found highly interesting.'

The exhibition was held in October in the upper room of the Exchange Arcade facing Lincoln's Cornhill, which gave more room and much easier access for the public, and was used until the First World War. Open for four days, the exhibition contained 172 pictures of which only five were sold. This was to prove a recurring problem over many decades. The largest was by Warrener, 'the Weir at Grez', with 'a daring foreground, cleverly achieved', according to the Gazette. Also praised were Mrs. Ruston's canvases of Johannesburg and Mentone, and Logsdail's 'remarkable, bold and brilliant' painting of the Grand Canal, Venice. Webster continued his series of Lincolnshire churches with Boston St. Botolph's and Saltfleet, and Miss Dering Curtois was to be commended for 'so attractively bringing before us the flower pickers of Lincolnshire'. Miss Pears, a noted flower painter, was now 'principally interested in artistic jewellery', representing perhaps the first showing of three-dimensional work.

1911

The only set of criticisms to be preserved in print from those early years came from the artist Mr. F Cayley-Robinson ROI, RBA, a noted muralist and illustrator, at the 1911 Exhibition. Avoiding looking at signatures in order to be impartial, he praised Warrener and the young George Boden, another product of Lincoln School of Art, but was direct with Major General Richardson, a prolific exhibitor, saying about his 'Calpe Hunt':

"I do not know much about hunting, but surely the hills are too steep for the horses?"

William Logsdail, *A Quiet Lane*

Several times he criticised the points of view from which scenes had been captured but of Webster's 'the South Coast', he said:

"This drawing is one of the best here. It has fine qualities of colour and design but over and above these, there is that sense of mystery which is characteristic of the best work of all times."

36 members heard Cayley Robinson speak out of a membership of 85, which for such a vast county is not a bad attendance, and 10 pictures were sold, doubling the sales of the previous year.

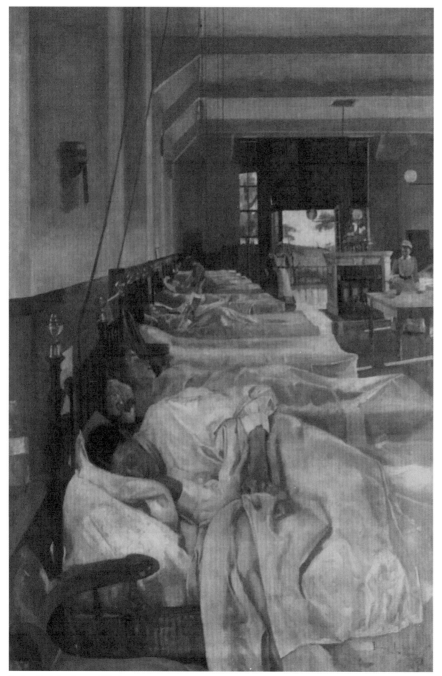

Dering Curtois, *Ruston Ward*

Lincolnshire Drawing Club.

FOUNDED 1906.

THE FIRST

ANNUAL EXHIBITION of DRAWINGS and PAINTINGS

Will be held **(by kind permission of Mr. J. S. RUSTON,)** at

MONKS MANOR,

On FRIDAY and SATURDAY, NOVEMBER 9th & 10th,

From 2 to 6 p.m. Each Day.

Managing Committee:

Miss ISOBEL HUTTON.   Mrs. AMCOTTS.

Miss A. SWAN.   Miss L. RICHARDSON.

Miss E. RUSTON, Hon. Sec.

First Invitation Card

1912 Honorary Members and a Change of Name

1912 was an outstanding year for the Drawing Club, because Logsdail and Bramley accepted its invitation to become honorary members alongside Lincoln-trained Joseph Bentley RBA, J.B. Kennington UPROI, G.E. Lodge, and Charles Shannon. At the October 30th General Meeting, Warrener proposed that the Club's name be changed to 'the Lincolnshire Artists' Society' and this was carried. It had become clear that with a widening membership and exhibitions of works in several media, the words 'drawing' and 'club' were too confining. Cecil Pilcher, an outstanding Marine artist from Boston, was welcomed onto the committee. The criticisms were given by Glasgow artist Alexander Jamieson R.O.I., who was invited back in 1913.

With an all-male roll of honorary members, the Lincolnshire Artists' Society also now had 16 male members including James Ward Usher the Lincoln jeweller, who had joined in 1910 and whose collection of furniture, clocks and watches was to form the backbone of the Usher Gallery from its opening in 1927. No fewer than 12 of the original female members were daughters, wives or sisters of clergymen in the Lincoln Diocese. These included the Misses Akenhead, Bourne, Craster, Curtois, Hutton, Jeudwine, Kaye, Melville, Long, Wickham and Blakesley. A Mrs. Gregorie of the Burghersh Chantry was on the Management Committee in 1908, while Miss Isobel Hutton of Vicar's Court became honorary treasurer in that year. Notably absent from the members' lists was a Miss Kirkland, the only local artist to offer 'lessons in drawing and painting' at her home in Clasketgate, which were announced on the 1908 front pages of the Echo. Perhaps she did not move in the Uphill circles of the Rustons and their aristocratic friends. But if the 1906 membership looked like a Who's Who of Uphill Lincoln, any such cliquishness had dissolved by 1912, when the membership doubled to 87 and included people from Sleaford, Grantham, Newark, Spilsby, Stamford, Louth and Woodhall Spa. The Lincolnshire Artists' Society, which we will now refer to as the LAS, was already on course to represent the entire county, and several notable artists from the Grimsby area had yet to appear.

1913

Alexander Jamieson returned to criticise the October 1913 Exhibition which nobody realised would be the last event of the LAS before the First World War. Indeed, at the AGM, the date of the 1914 Exhibition was set for the week of October 18th and two guest critics were proposed. But the first phase of the Society's history closed with a flourish of 213 exhibits which included a study of the Harlequin Inn on Steep Hill by George Boden, and several entries by Harold Coop, another Lincoln trained artist who was acquiring a good reputation for topographical and architectural work and who was to become a lecturer at Sheffield College of Art. There was the usual mixture of subjects from Scotland, Cornwall, Norfolk, Lincolnshire and abroad, and J.W. Usher submitted two paintings of his porcelain, while Miss Pears offered another case of her jewellery. It would be the last exhibition in the Corn Exchange Room. A

further three Honorary Members were proposed and added, but while A.G. Webster and his pupil Fred Elwell were enrolled in 1913, a Miss E. Beatrice Bland of Cheyne Walk Chelsea was nominated and approved in that year, but actually enrolled in 1918. She had studied at Lincoln School of Art and then at the Slade, and had been a founder member of the Society in 1906.

The Society was in good shape when the First World War broke out. 91 members were shown on the list of 1913, a handful with central London addresses, and the majority residing in Lincolnshire. No membership list is filed for 1914. but several strong links had been forged in the first seven years, the strongest being with the Lincoln School of Art. This link would flourish in decades to come, as would the link with London.

The Society's third strong link, and perhaps its most crucial was with the Lincolnshire press, which rarely failed to provide thorough and positive reviews, and even initiated or furthered healthy debate by printing adverse criticism from independent individuals. But all this would have to wait for a less deferential age.

2

Post-War Revival 1919-1926

Herbert Rollett, *Alexandra Dock*

Austin Garland, *The Kimono*

1919

The First World War put a stop to the activities of the Lincolnshire Artists' Society. Harold Coop gained the Military Cross as a commissioned officer and Frank Bramley died in 1915 after a crippling illness, aged only 58. When the Committee met for the first time in almost six years, on March 25th 1919, they concluded that things were too unsettled to reopen the Society for some months, with many of the Members still on War work.

Thus the date of re-opening was unresolved and it was decided to hold a General Meeting later in the year. Warrener was in the Chair as before, with Mrs. Herbert Mence as Secretary, Mrs. Mason as Treasurer, and Mrs. Gregorie and Mrs. Ruston completing the committee.

Discouraging Developments

December 11th 1919 saw the Special General Meeting take place at number one Mainwaring Road, Lincoln, the home of Mrs. Mence. Eleven ladies were present with George Boden, and Warrener was absent. It was decided to hold an exhibition in March 1920 and, 'if the Committee of the Free library will give their consent', to hold it there for one week. George Boden approached the library, and on January 9th 1920 the Committee, chaired by Warrener, accepted Mrs. Ruston's resignation and announced the exhibition dates of 8th - 20th March at the Public Library. Mrs. Gregorie was authorised to open a bank account for the Society. Then came a minute concerning membership:

> 'As a result of the circular sent out in Dec. 1919 to the Old Members (87), there were seven refusals to continue membership, 43 who wished to continue, and 37 no replies. Five new members were proposed and accepted.'

There was an even sadder note. A.G. Webster had recently died, and a 'special showing' of his work was to be included in the exhibition as a tribute. He had been Headmaster of Lincoln Art School for almost forty years, from 1877 to 1916. His retirement had been all too brief.

A New Home for Seven Years

Between 1920 and 1926 there would be seven exhibitions in Lincoln's new Central Library on Free School Lane, which opened in 1914. Lawrence Elvin states in 'Lincoln As It Was,' Vol. II, that the room housing the Reference Library was used for exhibitions, and he featured a photograph of art works rather densely hung on its walls. Apart from a difference of opinion with various Aldermen about charging schoolchildren to see the LAS exhibitions, things seemed to have gone smoothly. The Society clearly needed money, so it charged 6d for adults and 3d for schoolchildren, and it was pointed out to the library committee that the Society had experienced 'some difficulty in getting housed'. It was felt ungracious to press the idea of free entry.

1920

The first exhibition in the library was from March 8th – 20th 1920 and John Wheatley was the critic. A Slade tutor at the time, he was in the New English Art Club and would become Director of the South African National Gallery and finally Director of the Sheffield Art Galleries between 1938 and 1947. He was presented with only 94 exhibits, but there were over 1000 visitors. Whether the reported 494 schoolchildren were included in that total is not clear, but the 19 paintings by Webster, loaned by several members, were much appreciated. The 'Echo' writer paid tribute to his 'versatility, depth of feeling and inspiring personality' and felt that the very high standard of the watercolours in the exhibition eclipsed the oil paintings in quality. Miss Lynn and Miss Pears had tackled the interiors of local churches with distinction, while Logsdail's 'Carnival Morning in Venice' was 'much in demand for reproduction'. George Boden's 'Tunisian Water Carrier' was felt to be very striking. But Warrener was not producing much new work. He exhibited an oil of the 'Moulin Rouge', and 'Day Dreams' showing a girl on a sunlit hillside, both having been exhibited and 'favoured' at the Paris Salon. Harold Coop and a new member Mr. R. Sharpe had produced several street scenes of Lincoln which were highly praised. Almost all the press notices thus far had mentioned Warrener before everyone else, and he would continue to be the Society's figurehead for many years to come, but a new Headmaster had arrived at Lincoln School of Art, who would dominate the Society for twenty years…

George Boden, *Staple Inn, Holborn*

Enter Austin Garland

The LAS lost no time in extending to Austin Garland its invitation to become an honorary member, and to sit on the committee. Garland was a Liverpool-born and trained painter who had taught at Liverpool Art School before becoming second Master at Dudley School of Art. He then succeeded Webster at Lincoln. Within a year (1921-22) he had succeeded Mrs. Gregorie as Secretary, and had invited his colleague at the School of Art, Mr. Alexander Grieve Kennedy, to join. Garland then proposed the formation of a Studio Committee (the first of several attempts) to acquire a studio where members could meet and work, and he assisted George Boden with the Society's publicity.

Austin Garland, *Portrait of a Man*

Norah Wright, *Sheep*

A Clash of Personalities

The Society's minutes give no hint of the tensions which must have existed between Garland and Warrener, but Garland actually instructed his students not to take any notice of 'that man'. A strict Catholic who went to see the Pope, Garland did not approve of the nude studies resulting from Warrener's time as a member of Toulouse-Lautrec's Bohemian circle in Paris. Later on, when Warrener's sister burned a lot of his work, Garland assisted her, and so effective was his edict against

Warrener that people could actually wander into Lincoln's antique shops to be told, if they spotted and liked a painting by Warrener, that they could take it away without charge! Nor did Garland stop at Warrener. One Saturday morning he discovered his colleague Kennedy in the Art School, engaging in a passionate embrace with a life-model, and sacked him on the spot. As a result Kennedy lost his home and his family and was forced to take cheap lodgings wherever he could find them. He had, however, adopted an exhibiting name, 'A Maculric',

Cecil Pilcher, *In The Trawlers Dock*

and perhaps came to feel that this might focus attention on the merits of his work rather than on his reputation. A proud Scot, he could be very boastful with his students, but as an artist, he was highly regarded.

1921 When Other Helpers Fail

In Lincoln, with traditional modes of representation flourishing at the Society's exhibitions, there would have been no problem with the various outbreaks of Cubism

and other types of Modernism occurring in London amongst the Bloomsbury artists and the Vorticists. No problem, that is, until 1921, when the Lincolnshire Echo writer felt the need to warn artists and public. In the report on the LAS's 1921 Exhibition, he said:

"There are however some phases of the new school of art which do not appeal to all. Take for instance the Impressionists and the Cubists. There may be much

Bernard Eyre-Walker *Crowland (Etching)*

in their technique which appeals to a select few, but not to the community as a whole, not to those who like something pleasing to look upon."

Apparently, some examples of this 'modern school' with its 'perverted ideas of beauty' had now crept in, but their perpetrators were not named. As usual, Warrener's work was singled out. "When other Helpers Fail", a sentimental subject depicting a beleaguered husband and wife, carried perhaps some significance for Warrener, as the Chairman of a depleted Society into whose midst had just come Austin Garland, his opposite in so many ways. And Garland's work was mentioned and praised immediately after Warrener's. Even worse, the reviewer had said 'one could not but regret that (Warrener) has of late not given us much of his work'. It was left to George Boden and a group of talented ladies to save the day. Boden's sojourn in North Africa would yield much subject matter over the next few years and in 1921 his 'Nuit Orientale' was praised for its 'wonderful picturisation of Oriental fantasies by night', while Miss Hogarth, Miss Pears and Mrs. Mason were praised, and Miss Nora Wright's Sicilian scenes were deemed to show 'talent of a high order'. A Mr. Hatton of Armstrong College, Newcastle, was the critic, and while there is no record, yet again, of his remarks, the Echo felt that the standard had markedly improved.

1922 'Fewer Pictures But Better Work'…

Thus ran the Echo's headline for the review of April 18th. Only 60 pictures were shown but an established marine artist from Boston, Dr. Cecil Pilcher, had joined the Society and his 'several fine watercolours' including 'Gravesend Pier' were 'extraordinarily fine' with 'quite masterly' breadth. It was noted that several key members were abroad or occupied by London exhibitions, but Logsdail showed his large oil of 1880, 'St. Anne's Almshouses, Antwerp,' which was deemed 'most imposing'. Earlier Warrener, too, trawled his back catalogue and came up with 'Le Lavoir', a huge oil about women doing their washing. Austin Garland showed a watercolour of St. John's Bridge, Tewkesbury, and the Rev. Norton Howe showed 'some excellent drawings' including 'Fiesole' and 'Before the Procession at Bruges'. Miss Pears was reckoned to be 'a conspicuous exponent of the new English School of still life painting'. Finally, another new member, Mr. T.G. Storey, showed 'advancement', and would, rather comically, continue to show advancement for several years. In 1923 we find him 'making great strides', while in 1924 he 'makes further advances every year'. There is no record of the identity of any critic for the 1922 Exhibition.

1923

The Society's Eleventh Exhibition was, in the Echo's opinion, a proof that 'the active local members are doing better work and improving and raising the standard year by year'. There were more exhibits, although no total is recorded. Alexander Kennedy's work was described as 'brilliant', while Garland had made 'two important efforts' and Boden had shown 'two of his oriental fantasies'. Pilcher's work, 'Thames Mud and Wharves' and 'Old Limehouse', both watercolours, were 'remarkably fine'. Miss Gertrude Harrison's study of an Old Man was 'remarkable for breadth of treatment', and Mrs. P. M. Young of Woodhall Spa had shown 'a harmonious' view of Haltham Court, while Mr. G. R. Morton of Louth had revealed a 'close study of atmospheric effects'.

Again, no critic is recorded, but at the AGM the Royal College of Art's Principal W. Rothenstein was yet again urged as a future critic along with two women – Laura Knight and Anna Airy. Miss Airy did come eventually in 1944, but then she enjoyed a long life.

1924 'The Grimsby Grocer' takes the limelight

The Twelfth Exhibition, reviewed in the Echo on May 17th, was notable as the first occasion on which Herbert Rollett of Grimsby exhibited with the Society. Born near Gainsborough in 1872 and virtually self-taught, he ran a grocery business called The Five 'O'Clock Tea Store, in Grimsby. He had already showed paintings all over Britain, in the Royal Scottish Academy, the Walker Art Gallery Liverpool, the Royal Institute of Oil Painters, and in Birmingham. Now, after successes at the Paris Salon and in the Royal Academy, he would exhibit many works in Lincoln in the final years up to his early death at 60 in 1932. The Echo enthused:

> "Mr. Rollett's 'Yorkshire Mill', with a distant view of the Humber remarkable for its truthfulness, aerial perspective and technique…the Grimsby Grocer – Artist… has a picture in this year's Academy."

Rollett's friendship with the great Nottingham painter Sir John Arnesby Brown RA probably began, as Rollett's biographer Allen Smith says, after Rollett worked as a shop manager in Nottingham. They painted together on summer holidays in the Gorleston area and a feeling of

Cecil Pilcher, *Boston May Fair*

breadth and dramatic lighting through clouds and over the sea characterise the work of both men, although Brown was also a distinguished painter of animals. But Rollett's handling of paint was in itself masterly, approaching the standard of Monet on some occasions, and his solo exhibitions in Lincoln, when he exhibited between 40 and 80 paintings, laid him open to criticisms of his 'sombre aura' and his 'reliance on the sky'. The important thing, as far as the Society was concerned,

was that in Rollett they had an active and prolific painter of real stature, who did not rely on past glories and who depicted the landscape of his home county with the same dedication that Constable had given to Dedham Vale. The Society would cherish Herbert Rollett until his death – and long afterwards.

Other highlights of the 1924 Exhibition included Nora Wright's watercolours produced during her stay in India,

'Storm in the Kashmir Hills' and other titles uniting the visual languages of India and Britain, and Dr. Pilcher's watercolours of the Thames which revealed 'a gift for investing its tidal reaches with beauty, atmosphere, and interest'. There was also the first architectural contribution from Mr. A. Hill, the Lincoln City Architect, who showed 'four excellent schemes for the improvement of Lincoln 'expressed most artistically'. Apparently his plans for the Brayford, St. Giles and Waterside repaid close study. The inclusion of architectural schemes in the Society's exhibitions would flourish from 1952 but it is interesting to see the seeds being sown in 1924.

1925

With Alexander Kennedy now an honorary member and T.G. Storey standing in for an indisposed Warrener, questions of finance began to dominate the Society's meetings. Subscription arrears occasioned a resolution that if members did not pay after receiving a notice from the treasurer, they would be struck off. And it was felt that 'the low financial state of the Society' was such that a critic could not be funded. The silver lining came when the Annual Exhibition was pronounced in the Echo of Oct. 5th to have a 'standard higher than ever'. The Exhibition had been deferred to the autumn to 'accommodate the illness of Mr. Warrener', who did not, in the end, submit any work, but whose health was reported to be improving. The 'Grimsby Grocer' showed three fine landscapes and Miss Nora Wright was now described as 'a well-known exponent of the Modern School' with her flower studies. Miss Pears' 'Castle at Chillon' was felt to be 'reminiscent of Webster' and Austin Garland showed a popular portrait of Bob Brown, the licensee of Lincoln's Lion and Snake. But the star of the year was the new honorary member Mr. Bernard Eyre-Walker, (a member of the Royal Society of Painters, Etchers and Engravers), who showed 'remarkably fine etchings and aquatints including 'Boston bridge at Low Tide'.

1926 The Usher Gallery is built

The Gossip Column of the Echo declared on Nov. 27th that the Usher Gallery, bequeathed to the City of Lincoln by James Ward Usher and designed by Sir Reginald Blomfield, was nearing completion. For several years Usher's watercolours of his collection had featured in the LAS exhibitions. A.R. Corns, the Lincoln librarian who had overseen the arrangements for all of the recent exhibitions in the Central library, would transfer to the Usher and continue to help the Society by programming time and gallery space for its annual exhibitions, and providing help from the gallery's new staff. The public, meanwhile, felt that while the building itself was admirable, the significance of the carved frieze of ox skulls escaped them and had nothing to do with the new art gallery or its founder. But Blomfield was a scholarly man, and knew that his frieze would have to feature bucrania, as the ox-skulls were called, in order to be classically correct!

With an Eye to Patronage

At the June 1926 Committee meeting, chaired by Storey, Miss Yeomans tendered her resignation as Treasurer, bequeathing a balance of only £6.6.0d. This was done by letter because of illness and Austin Garland was instructed to convey the Committee's sympathies and asked to take on the Treasurership. He was also instructed to write to Sir Hickman Bacon, Premier Baronet of England and Lincolnshire landowner, and Sir Archibald and Lady Weigall of Petwood House, Woodhall Spa, to invite them to become Honorary Members, for a fee of ten shillings. Intriguingly, no more is heard from the Weigalls (whose wealth, though fabled, was being stretched in other directions) but Sir Hickman Bacon, with a superb art collection, did become involved and was even elected President of the Society in October 1943. The Society's last exhibition in the Library took place in November 1926, and Garland's Accounts reveal that a critic was paid the usual £5, but records of the exhibition are missing. In future, no catalogue would ever go missing, for from 1927 to the present day, all are filed in the Usher Yearbooks. With Warrener re-elected as Chairman for the next phase of the Society's life, its first, rather nomadic, period was over, and it could at last look forward to exhibitions in a fine new purpose-built gallery, where the focus would begin to shift towards debates about art.

New Home, New Problems 1927-39

Fred Elwell, *Bric a Brac*

Ernest Worrall, *Snow At Healing, Lincolnshire*

Public expectations are raised whenever art is exhibited inside any major art gallery. The feeling is that the art should live up to the building, and this was to lead to a number of problems for artists and public alike when the LAS exhibited at Lincoln's new Usher Gallery – problems which would not have arisen in the Society's nomadic days when they gratefully exhibited in any available space and were greeted by an equally grateful press and public.

1927 saw the opening of the Usher Gallery in Lincoln, the Ferens Art Gallery in Hull, and the birth of the St. Ives Society of Artists in Cornwall. The St. Ives Society did not have the enthusiasm or confidence with which the Lincolnshire Drawing Club had started out, for St. Ives was then a much depleted art colony and it was hoped that a Society might bring artists together, raise standards, and promote art in St. Ives in a time of national depression. Yet even at its first AGM, a motion was put forward that the Society should terminate! No such negativity has ever afflicted the LAS, despite many problems.

Considering that the Society had just mounted its first ever exhibition in the new Usher Gallery, the Echo's

Charles Shannon, *The Capture*

Charles Shannon, *The Toilet*

review of October 19th was surprisingly brief, but it does at least hint that the exhibits were well hung:

> "Thanks to Mr. A. R. Corns and his staff the pictures can be seen to best advantage."

Corns, the Librarian at Lincoln, was also now in charge of the Usher, providing continuity for the Society's committee, who recorded grateful thanks to him and to his staff.

A Pocket of Turbulence

Fear of the modern reared its head yet again as the Echo reviewer continued;

> "Ultra-modern works have very little representation, and judging from a conspicuous example, one is heartily thankful that this is so."

This problem would not go away, but in 1927 the mixture was very much the same as usual. Boden still mined his North African vein with 'In Old Tunis', while honorary member Charles Shannon's 'Artist at Work' and Garland's portrait of Monsignor William Croft were felt to be excellent. John R. Lewis, ARCA, a Lincoln man then living in South Wales, showed two watercolours deemed 'well above the average' while Mr. James Dawson's 'Light at Eventide, Sutton Marsh', was thought 'particularly arresting'. Mrs. Mason's work was also praised. But if this brief notice does not sound as exciting as previous reviews, there may have been a good reason.

1928

After the 1928 Exhibition, the Echo printed letters which questioned the standard of work. A correspondent called 'Nix', later identified as a Mr. Gill, said many of the pictures were badly drawn, lacked depth, and bore inflated price-tags. No response was forthcoming so 'Nix' wrote again and this time was supported by 'a lover of Art' who had been disgusted by the LAS exhibits for several years and thought that membership of the Society was based not on being a genius but on belonging to a certain clique in Lincoln.

Garland, Rollett and a professor from Chelsea Art School replied to 'Nix', challenging his assertions. Rollett maintained that the 1928 exhibition had been the best seen in Lincoln for some years, but then he had contributed four landscapes including 'Salt Marshes on the Norfolk Coast'. Meanwhile three outstanding artists in the Society (Elwell, Boden and Storey) were given solo shows at the Usher in that same year.

If 'Nix' and the 'lover of Art' were referring to the amateur members, they may have overlooked the fact that all members were still given a criticism by a well known artist before each exhibition. The Society's Accounts, now neatly typed by Austin Garland, record fees for critics every year, even if the critic who eventually came to Lincoln is rarely identified from shortlists, which included names like William Nicholson, Laura Knight and William Rothenstein. In 1927 the critic was W.C. Penn, but the critic for 1928 is not known.

1929 Enter Judith Oyler

On December 7th the Society's AGM elected as a member a young woman from Devon who had come to Lincoln to teach art at the Girls' High School. Born in Worcestershire and art-trained in Grimsby, Judith Oyler would remain one of the staunchest members for 54 years until her death in 1983. Forthright, deep-voiced and humorous, she worked in a variety of media and even taught leatherwork in the evenings. Always referred to as 'Miss Oyler', she was the first of several strong-minded and deeply committed women who would occupy top positions in the Society, shaping policy and maintaining standards. She was no 'prima donna'

regarding her own work, but she could be very scathing about 'modern art' and she produced excellent landscape watercolours which rather contradicted the severity of her outer personality.

Meanwhile Miss Dering Curtois, a founder member, had died in 1928 in her mid-seventies. Her watercolours had always been mentioned and consistently praised by the Press, and the Society sent a wreath to her funeral. In 1929 the Usher held a memorial exhibition of her paintings and drawings. The Annual Exhibition was held from October 9th – November 9th but there was no report about it in the Society's records. There was also an exhibition of the work of the great portraitist Gerald Kelly.

1930 A Touch of Diplomacy

With Warrener restored to health and back in the chair, the 1920's drew to a close with meetings at the Usher or the School of Art, and in 1930 at the May 24th Committee meeting we find that a letter from Dr. Pilcher complained about the way his pictures had been hung by the gallery staff, the first recorded instance of discontent since Rollett had suggested in 1928 that the hanging left a little to be desired. Garland was instructed to reply as follows:

> *"The Committee regrets that Dr. Pilcher has found it necessary to complain of the manner in which his pictures were presented for Exhibition, and beg to assure him that the matter will be brought to the notice of the Gallery Authorities."*

On a contrasting note, Garland was also asked to convey compliments to Harold Coop, who had a painting accepted in the Royal Academy, but the committee's sympathy on his illness was also conveyed, and sadly he died later that year, aged only 39. The outcome of Pilcher's complaint is not recorded, but at the first AGM of many to be held at the Eastgate Court Café, on Dec 6th, a vote of thanks was 'unanimously accorded to the Art Gallery Committee and Mr. A.R. Corns for the use of the Gallery and the assistance rendered to the Society in connection with the Annual Exhibition.' It seems any tensions had been laid to rest.

The Social Dimension – Tea with the President

The Eastgate Court Café was clearly the favourite venue for most Society meetings in the 1930's and this suggests that members needed a more neutral ground which would provide refreshments as an accompaniment to a little more socialising. At that first café gathering there seemed plenty to celebrate; for it was resolved that Warrener should become the Society's first President, and should hold office for three years and be eligible for re-election. One wonders what Garland made of this, for the President would be the 'Chief Officer', but the agenda was packed, and it was recorded that efforts should be made to circulate the Annual Exhibition through the Principal Towns of the County, and that a sale of pictures for the benefit of the County Hospital Building Fund should be arranged. Garland then left the meeting, returning 15 minutes later to be told he had been voted an honorarium of five guineas. He 'objected to the principle' of receiving 'any such sum', but 'eventually accepted', and thanked the meeting 'with a few appropriate words.'

Warrener, now President, invited members to remain to tea as his guests, and the meeting closed after Garland, no doubt mollified by his five guineas, was 'instructed' to thank the man who, by all accounts, he heartily disliked. How very English that clashing personalities could at least meet, for a moment, over a pot of tea!

The Annual Exhibition of 1930 was held from October 11th to November 9th in the Usher, the critic being Gilbert Spencer, the brother of Stanley Spencer and a considerable artist in his own right. Unusually, the Echo review actually named him, but said nothing new or unusual about the exhibits.

1931 A Mysterious Criticism

Garland's handwriting is often indecipherable but some passages are remarkably clear, and one such concerned a minute about the criticism given to the 1931 Exhibitors by an unidentified guest.

The shortlist of critics was Walter Bayes, William Nicholson, Dame Laura Knight, Bernard Meninski and Glen Phillpot, and the minute read:

> 'The Secretary presented the shorthand writer's report of the criticisms, owing to the unsatisfactory nature of the report, the secretary was requested to write a report based on the shorthand notes, and read the same at the AGM, and notify members that a discussion will follow.'

The Annual Meeting of 1932 featured the discussion, and the meeting must have felt strongly about the criticism because it was resolved to circulate copies of Garland's report to all members. Even the Echo had found the exhibition of 1931 wanting, and said that 'the worst faults appear to be washiness in watercolours, and in some other exhibits a lack of good draughtsmanship.' But Eyre-Walker's 'Dawn in Langdale' was highly praised and Mrs. B. Young's watercolour of 'Kirkby Lane in Woodhall Spa' was 'less watery than some of the other watercolours shown'!

Meanwhile a young colleague of Garland's joined the Society. Bertram Batt was reckoned by many to be the best painter in the Art School, with an Indian mother and an English father. His name appears in several minutes but he didn't stay long in Lincoln and went on to work in Leeds, only to be killed in the D. Day Operations. T.G. Storey was now Chairman, only the second to be appointed so far, but Rollett's name had not featured for several meetings and in 1931 he fell seriously ill.

1932

The LAS responded generously to Rollett's plight and Storey convened a special meeting in April at which he

George Storey, *The Sanctuary*

Herbert Rollett dies…and Edward Brannan takes his place

The LAS was as good as its word and purchased a painting from Rollett, presumably shortly before he died in December. His final submission to the Annual Exhibitions had been in 1931: 'Morning Light', 'By the Humber' and 'The Close of Day'. He had served on the committee for several years, and in March 1933 the AGM at the Eastgate Court Café witnessed his name being removed and replaced with that of 'Mr. E. Brannan'. This was the first recorded mention of Edward Eaton Brannan in the LAS minutes. He had been a friend and student of Rollett's, having sketched and painted under his guidance at classes run privately by Rollett. Born in 1886, Brannan had been encouraged to paint by a scene painter at Grimsby theatre where his father had led the orchestra. He then went to North Shields to work in the Ministry of Agriculture and from then on his work was shown at the Laing Art Gallery in Newcastle, then at the Royal Academy, the Paris Salon and many other institutions. Starting out as an etcher, he began in 1926 an obsession with watercolour washes, which captured the subtleties of the Lincolnshire landscape, and it could have been his influence that upset the Echo reviewer when he had complained of 'washiness of watercolours', perhaps regarding this as a fault rather than a strength! Brannan was however, the ideal successor to Rollett, and his two sons Noel and Peter would also become members of the Society, Peter eventually becoming the President in 1993.

A Sculptural Element

Sculptural contributions to the Annual Exhibition had been rare. There had been some carved boxes, and Miss Pears' jewellery, but in 1932 we find Kathleen Hyett and Margaret Clark exhibiting 'plaster models' called 'Happy Dreams' and 'Joyce'. Then in 1933 a sculptor on the staff of the Art School, Mr. A. Willetts ARCA, who had accompanied Henry Moore on his famous early scholarship to Italy, also showed some plaster models.

detailed what had been done to assist Mr. Rollett. It was decided to appeal to members for funds so that one of Rollett's paintings could be purchased for the Usher, as a permanent exhibit. In any case, such moneys as were collected should be sent to Mrs. Rollett 'without delay to alleviate her present distress.'

E.E. Brannan, *Sky With A Shaft Of Light*

The Echo's reviewer merely noted the presence of these sculptures, without comment, and it may be that at this time, few provincial exhibitions actually featured sculpture.

George Boden was a clay modeller as well as an Orientalist painter, and in his 1937 exhibition at the Usher he showed several caricatures in clay of local celebrities, but he also made models of George Bernard Shaw, Hitler, G.K. Chesterton and Mussolini!

The 1932 Exhibition was back on form after the dismal showing of 1931. Herbert Rollett's daughter, Kathleen, contributed some watercolours which were praised along with Boden's usual oriental scenes, Garland's 'Scene in Jerusalem'. And Kathleen Tyson of Grimsby's 'The Road to Cassis'. Karl Wood, the notable Gainsborough artist, was now a member and received a mention for his 'soft-toned effects', while Judith Oyler's scenes of Bute were 'clever and original', and another Grimsby-area artist, E. J. Worrall ARCA, exhibited for the first time with 'three clever pieces', one being a most interesting windmill study. Worrall would become a prominent member of the Society, and was the art master at Wintringham School.

1933

With artists of the calibre of Brannan, Worrall and Wood as new members, the Society had strengthened and renewed itself, and was pleased to include the work of an eighteen year-old apprentice called K.P. Johnson, of Barton-on-Humber, in the Exhibition of 1933, held from October 7th to November 5th. Young Johnson had taken examples of his work to Hull Art College, where he asked for lessons, but was told to go home and carry on with his work there. The Echo detected 'great promise' in his work, which consisted of two oil paintings, 'Humber from the Wolds' and 'Low Tide at Staithes'.

Apart from this phenomenon the review was brief and eerily similar to several previous years. Fifteen members

E.J. Worrall, *Cold Bath House After War Damage, 1943*

met for the AGM at the Eastgate Court Café on March 25th and again the idea of the travelling exhibition was discussed, 'but no definite arrangements were made'!

1934 Obeying the Rules

Problems over subscriptions, and the selection of works for exhibitions, began to appear at this time and the January committee meeting heard that almost 30 members had not paid their subscriptions. George

Boden urged that 'a sharp reminder be sent to all defaulting members', but he then went on to utter the most arresting entry to be found in the Society's minutes – he suggested that 'stewards be appointed to control members' during the criticism! It is infuriating that in the next sentence Garland's writing deteriorates, but finally, the words 'stewards were not appointed' can be made out. It seems that the critical sessions were the occasions of some unrest, perhaps from members who took exception to what the critics were saying.

Putting the house in order

The hanging committee also warned that at the 1933 Exhibition, several works had been hung without its knowledge, and it was resolved strictly to enforce the rule that ALL work must be passed by the committee. Having given itself a good talking-to, the committee next turned on the Press, suggesting that in future someone outside the Society but in the art world should be invited to write an appreciative criticism suitable for publication. The Annual Exhibition was held from June 2nd to July 1st, an early summer show no doubt dictated by available time-slots at the Usher. At the preceding Annual Meeting in March, Kathleen Tyson was elected to the committee. She would eventually become the Society's first woman Chairman. A proposal that the press be invited to attend the criticisms was overwhelmingly defeated after an animated discussion.

W.T. Warrener Dies

It is astonishing that the death of the Society's first President, who was one of its founder members and its first Chairman, is not recorded in the Society's minutes. But it must be remembered that Garland was writing them, and others were agreeing to their accuracy, indicating that Garland could behave like those pharaohs who obliterated the names of hated predecessors from their monuments. We will never know what actually happened, but the Society may have wished to distance itself from the early days of Warrener's domination.

The year closed happily with a September meeting at the Usher, at which Borlase Smart, a founder of the St. Ives Society of Artists, spoke to 30 members of the LAS about progress in St. Ives. This gathering adjourned to the Eastgate Court Café for tea.

1935

With Boden once again in the Chair for the first meeting of the year, it was becoming clear that Storey was ill, and a malaise of the financial sort was also afflicting the Society, for as 1934 closed, it had only £3.5.10d in the kitty. The Exhibition was arranged for June but as an economy measure it was decided not to advertise it in the press. Elwell, Meninski and Frances Hodge were on the shortlist for critic. The question of the Presidency was raised (no doubt by Garland, since no other name is attached to this minute) but it was decided to refer to the absent Chairman. Whether Storey's view was ever obtained is not known, for he died later that year and a Special Meeting of October 5th decided to recommend Dr. Pilcher for the office of Chairman of the Society. That same day, the AGM welcomed Pilcher into the Chair and heard that there were now 90 members, three significant new ones being Miss Haggart ARCA, Miss I. Tate, and Catherine Spence-Whyte DA. Miss Spence-Whyte was the art tutor at the Diocesan Training College in Lincoln, and would become a prominent member. A brief mention was made of the cost of the wreath for Warrener - £4.6.0d – without mentioning his name. And Garland even questioned the need for any further Presidents, 'recalling the circumstances in which this office had been created'. As a result, the meeting decided that the office of president was 'no longer necessary'. Finally, reference was made to Mr. Francis Cooper, Mr. Corns' successor.

1936

Francis Cooper's name appears without fanfare on November 29th 1936, when Pilcher announced the deaths of two more 'very active' members, Messrs. Dawson and Tipping. The Exhibition opened on June

20th – clearly the Usher was finding it convenient to put the LAS in an early summer slot – and Norman Wilkinson was asked to criticise the work, but there is no record of his visit. It seems that fewer sales resulted from the earlier date, because Boden proposed (November 28th) that in future the exhibition 'should be held in October as formerly'. Statistics on sales, comparing Junes to Octobers in the past, were considered and Boden's proposal was carried narrowly.

The Midland Federation of Art Societies

Until 1936 the LAS had existed in isolation, attracting members from all over the County, so when Mr. J. R. Park drew the Society's attention to the Midland Federation of Art Societies, and asked why the Society had not been affiliated, Garland was instructed to write to the Federation, and Mr. Park was appointed correspondent. Francis Cooper was made Secretary of the special sub-committee set up to circularise members and advise them regarding the submission of work to the Federation's exhibitions.

1937

The Society held an October Exhibition at the Usher, in a year which recorded only one meeting - a committee meeting on February 3rd. The guest critic was probably Norman Wilkinson, and a critic's fee is mentioned in the accounts, but again there is no recorded outcome to the invitation made to him. The LAS paid its dues to the Midland Federation, George Boden continued to show his Orientalist watercolours, and it seems that the press began to lose interest, for there would be no further reviews until 1942, even though bold headlines welcomed many other Usher exhibitions, and began to follow Nevile Chamberlain's dealings with Germany, with a mixture of hope and trepidation.

1938 Economy Measures

With Francis Cooper now on the Committee of the Midland Federation of Art Societies, it is hardly surprising that the Usher was booked as the 1938 venue for the Federation's exhibition, during April and May. Contrasting with this expansive development which would involve interested members of the LAS, the Society's AGM endorsed an idea put forward by Pilcher and Garland that instead of having a critic, the two men would give an informal criticism at the Annual Exhibition on September 17th, followed by a discussion. This would be 'an experiment' – but it would also save the critic's fee of five guineas – a sum which had not risen, and which in real terms had dramatically lessened - since 1907!

There was also talk of expenses being saved by issuing a 'simpler booklet', the contents of which are not made clear. It also seems that the Press were not made aware of the Exhibition, for no review can be traced in the Echo, and there was an immediate reaction to the informal, in-house criticism of 20 members who attended a meeting immediately after it – they urged that 'an outside critic be asked to criticise the exhibits' of the next Exhibition! In the event, it seems no critic came, but in October 1939 the Second World War had just broken out, and the Society's accounts for that year give no commission figure on sales, no critic's fee, and catalogue costs. A careful examination of the Usher's Yearbook does not even offer a catalogue. But an exhibition was scheduled and could have taken place with a typewritten list of the exhibits which has long since vanished. In wartime, typed lists would become the norm. The interwar years may have closed with a whimper, but one new face refreshed the Society's subject matter…

Enter Peter Scott

With Dr. Pilcher honoured with an OBE, a young man who was his equal in watery subjects, Peter (later Sir Peter) Scott, showed several wildfowl watercolours in the 1938 Exhibition. The son of Robert Falcon Scott of the Antarctic, Peter had trained at the Royal Academy Schools and his first solo exhibition had been in 1933. In 1936 he had represented Britain in the Olympics as a single-handed dinghy racer. He had a London address but he also lived by the River Nene near Gedney Drove End in an old lighthouse. Scott was actually enrolled as a member in 1946. Judith Oyler seems to have fallen beneath Pilcher's spell, for in 1940 she moved from her Somerset and Devon subjects of 1938 to some 'boats in harbour' and even entered Pilcher's special territory with 'On the Thames'. Pilcher showed a 'Swedish Schooner' in the 1940 Exhibition when Boden, not to be outdone in the water stakes, exhibited 'Millpond, Swanage'. Then in 1939, all was silence and uncertainty. But Francis Cooper and his assistant Monica Smith would look after the LAS throughout the Second World War, and witness its First Golden Age, which is the subject of the next chapter.

National Recognition and Jubilee Celebrations
1940-59

Judith Oyler, *Lights Over Lincoln*

1940

Despite the temporary suspension of the Society's annual Criticisms, the Exhibitions themselves went ahead during the first four years of the Second World War. New members broadened the range of work and while many younger members were involved in the armed forces, some of the women were active in the Civil Defence, Judith Oyler joining the Lincoln First Aid Party, while a new member in 1940, Miss Mary Dudding, was dedicated to working with the Red Cross. Mary Dudding had trained at Norwich School of Art and had executed some fine etchings, wood engravings and aquatints. In the 1940 Exhibition from May to June, she showed a watercolour of the River Yare and an embroidered panel, and, in 1942, some drawings of period costumes. Highly strung and easily stirred to indignation if her work was not chosen by hanging committees, she was nonetheless generous and party-loving in her earlier days. Her brother was the diplomat, Sir John Dudding, who lived at Winteringham. She became quite a character around Uphill Lincoln, living in a comfortable house off Greestone Terrace.

Another new member, a Lincoln photographer with studio premises on St. Mary's Street, was Lance Holtby. He was a watercolourist, and became well known for the Lincolnshire scenes he exhibited with the LAS, beginning in 1940 with a watercolour of 'The Mayor's Chair', the conveniently placed seat halfway up Steep Hill. His versatility is shown in an oil he exhibited in 1945 called 'Chinese Lanterns'.

Austin Garland, Pilcher, Boden, and the Misses Oyler and Tyson made a strong showing throughout the War and there were some fascinating exhibitions from other sources at the Usher, including watercolours by Czechoslovakian Artists in 1940, and works by the St. Ives Society in 1944. Such varied activities and exhibits must have made up for low numbers of accepted entries for LAS members. In 1940 there were 98 exhibits, but they plummeted to 55 in 1941, the lowest number ever,

Mary Dudding, *The Late Canon A.M. Cook*

to climb slowly back to 71 in 1942. But in 1945 there was a massive 282 exhibits.

1941 – 42 Severe Cutbacks

There had been a neat, printed joint-catalogue for the 1940 Exhibition of the work of George Boden, which included his cartoons, caricatures and posters. But in 1941, savings had to be made and a simple typewritten list of the 55 exhibits was issued, and rather pathetically entitled 'Exhibition of Work by Some Members of the LAS'. A new name on this list was G.W. Bailey FRSA, who showed watercolours of Boston and the Menai Straits. There was no local press review, but in 1942 the Echo sent someone to the Exhibition on October 19th

Mary Dudding, *Rocking Horse - Version II*

who noted only 'One war picture in the Lincs. Artists' Array', by H. White, called 'The Casualty'. Boden, Pilcher and Miss Oyler were praised, as were Miss Dudding's costume designs. The 'array' consisted of 71 exhibits, detailed yet again on a sheet of paper.

1943 Wartime Conditions

With only 39 effective members recorded for this year, it is a tribute to the Society that it managed to exhibit 81 works, with 'the collection of works by A. Garland' to be used 'for circulation to various ATS units'. Subscriptions for members serving in the Armed Forces had been suspended and there was a note of a 'Donation to the Artists' Benevolent Fund' of two guineas. Garland presented a report on the state of the Society at the AGM on October 30th, when only 8 people were present. It had been noted however that transport difficulties made it impossible for people like E. E. Brannan to attend. Meanwhile, Boden announced the sad death of Dr. Pilcher.

Judith Oyler, *Road In The Marsh*

Big Decisions

The 1943 AGM took several decisions which would affect the Society profoundly in the future. Garland stood down as Hon. Secretary and Treasurer, preparing the way for Francis Cooper to begin a memorable and lengthy period as his successor. Cooper would be helped by the indispensable Monica Smith, who would eventually succeed him as the Usher's Keeper in 1964. It was resolved that henceforth the Chairman should be elected for a term of one year and that the Deputy Chairman should automatically succeed. And Presidents were clearly back in vogue, after the Society had so emphatically voted to do away with the office, for Sir Hickman Bacon, Bt., was elected as the Society's second President. On the committee were the ever reliable E. E. Brannan and the Rev. Canon Norton Howe

as well as Miss A. King, one of the Society's founder members, and the Misses Oyler and Tyson. After various tributes to Pilcher and Garland, Garland was elected to the Chair and 'at the rise of the meeting tea was served'.

1944 Associate Memberships Begin

A momentous minute of the Special General Meeting of May 26th ran:

> *"New members: The Secretary announced the names of new Associate Members under the new rules."*

It had been resolved in April that the Associates would have their submissions for exhibitions adjudicated by the hanging committee. Not all Associates were practicing artists, however, and Judith Oyler tried several times to question their right to attend the criticism, which suggests that she felt Full Members deserved privacy when their work was being dissected. Several members agreed, but in May 1945 her resolution was defeated. Being a very strict schoolmistress, she perhaps felt that young people (the minutes reveal Associates paid different rates depending on whether they were over or under 18) should not partake in situations which could prove embarrassing for mature members. By 1945, there were 75 Associate Members, setting a trend in which they would outnumber Full Members. The Special Meeting of May 20th was attended by a very encouraging 24 people, and for the first time, the names of all three Brannans, father and two sons, are recorded as present. The Meeting concurred with Miss Tyson's view that the Annual Exhibitions should be much better publicised, and Miss Tyson conveyed the wish of the North Lincolnshire Artists' Society to be affiliated with the LAS, while a Mr. Clark spoke in similar terms on behalf of the Boston Arts and Crafts Society.

An Exhibition of Great Variety

On June 24th it was decided that a selection of Dr. Pilcher's paintings should be shown as a memorial to him alongside the Annual Exhibition for October 25th.

Anna Airy, ROI, RI, RE, was the guest artist and critic and there would be a small exhibition of 15 of her works. This was the first and, until 2001, the only instance of a woman being asked to fill this role. Miss Airy had a lot to consider, for there were 171 two-dimensional exhibits, a large number of plaster portrait plaques by Professor Artur Loewental, and several miniatures by Elsie Birkett. Artur Loewental, a native of Vienna, but resident in London since 1934, had already had a solo exhibition at the Usher in December 1941, in which his relief portraits of Einstein, Rudyard Kipling, Van Hindenberg and the Duchess of Devonshire had been shown. John Grimble, a recent Associate Member, showed a female torso carved from teak. Mr. Grimble would prove a hard-working member of the Society in the decades to come, as would Gilbert Farrow of Lytham St. Anne's, who became Chief Fisheries and Pollution Officer to the Lincolnshire River Authority. He also joined in 1944, aged only 34, and would inspire the affection of members until his early death in 1966.

1945 Francis Cooper's Album

The LAS found in Francis Cooper a passionate advocate and careful historian. From 1945 to 1960 he kept a vivid album of cuttings and Annual Reports, charting the Society's rise to national recognition. His pride in the Society leaps from every page, but he acknowledged every year the equally devoted help of Miss Monica Smith, his assistant at the Usher. She helped all the exhibitors, and could be rather fierce, but she 'knew everyone' and was always there, allowing Cooper to bask in the limelight while she continued to be indispensable.

A Boston Tea Party

1945 was a packed year. Garland's offer of studio facilities at the School of Art was eagerly taken up and the monthly gathering worked from life-models and had discussions over tea. The attendance averaged 25, not bad for a scattered membership. The first cycle of summer excursions was inaugurated with a day in Boston at the invitation of the Boston Arts and Crafts Society when their members showed the LAS (46 of them) the sights of the town, held a civic reception in the Guildhall, and provided tea. The LAS organised a successful Victory Poster Competition for Lincolnshire Schools and there were over 500 entries. 23 awards were made and Woolworth's gave a top prize. The results were exhibited at the Usher and the event was opened by the Rt. Hon. Captain H.F.C. Crookshank, the Society's new President. Sir Hickman Bacon had died, and so had the Rev. Norton Howe. There had been a successful first meeting with the Lincoln Camera Club, at which Worrall had presented the case for painting, and some amusing argument followed.

An Outstanding Exhibition and a County Tour

Francis Hodge, the distinguished Devon-born Portraitist, was the guest artist and critic for the Annual Exhibition of 1945 opened on October 25th. It had more exhibits than ever before – 282 entries from 114 exhibitors. There were 12 sales and well over 6000 visitors. Enhancing the LAS's aspirations to 'encourage appreciation of Art in the County', the Lindsey and Holland Rural Community Council enabled 69 of the works shown in the Usher to tour to Boston, Holbeach, Spalding, Louth, Horncastle, Spilsby and Donington.

The Studio Fund

Another aspiration was given shape in the form of Cooper's exhortation to members to contribute to a fund for the eventual purchase of a Society Studio, an idea which had been around for some time. Cooper stressed the advantage of being able to leave paintings on easels undisturbed, and felt that visitors would welcome a convenient place to meet members. But the members were never able (or disposed) to donate the amount needed to purchase a property, despite Cooper's assertion that it need not be 'an elaborate premises'. Disappointment would dog this project, until it spluttered

Marchbank Salmon, *The White Yacht*

out and re-ignited as the Judith Oyler Memorial Prize, decades later. But, in 1945, at least Boden could see the advantages of a Society studio, and donated three guineas!

The many activities outlined above continued for many years leaving space here for only the briefest mention of outstanding events, for it is time to address the Society's growing stature, reflected in the evidence of its guest critics.

1946 Adrian Hill recommends 'the Innocent Eye'

George Boden became Chairman in November 1945 after Garland stepped down, and it was his pleasant duty to introduce to the assembled members at the Opening of the 1946 Exhibition on October 25th, the Vice President of the Royal Society of British Artists, Adrian Hill. This urbane and striking individual would become BBC television's 'Sketch Club' presenter, and after 1951, when most of the country received transmissions, his name became almost a household word. In his speech at the Usher, he recounted some amusing stories but made a strong and helpful point when he said the most important factor in the making of a picture was 'the innocent eye'. He felt it was disastrous to approach a subject with a preconceived idea of exactly how one would carry it out. One must experiment and get rid of mannerism. He then discussed several chosen examples from the exhibition, praising forthrightness, calm assurance and strength of design.

The affiliated societies showed groups of work in the third room available to the LAS, which for the first time had less space at its disposal because of the permanent installation of the De Wint collection in a large room formerly used for temporary exhibitions. Loewental continued to show portrait medals, and the Chronicle reviewer thought the watercolours to be of a very high standard.

Peter Scott reappears in the minutes as a 'New Member' despite first exhibiting with the LAS in the late thirties, and so does David Tarttelin of Grimsby who was to become a distinguished sporting painter. The young Tarttelin had a surprise or two up his sleeve for the forthcoming exhibitions, submitting a startling pastel of the 'Baptism of Our Lord', which showed Christ as a negro, in 1949.

1947 Farewell to Austin Garland

Lord Brownlow of Belton House had become a Vice President of the LAS and, in common with Lord Yarborough, had invited the Society to his home to sketch

or to relax. During the early June visit, Boden made a presentation to Garland and his wife of a silver cigarette box on a tray with a lighter attached, to mark his retirement from the School of Art, the Society, and from Lincoln itself. Cooper's letter to members spoke of Garland's 24 years of devotion to the LAS and to art in Lincoln. He retired to Wales but continued to exhibit with the LAS. His successor at the School of Art would be the immaculately dressed Scot, James Marchbank Salmon, whose name was first wrongly recorded as Marchmont Salmond! He was of course invited to join the LAS, and he exhibited Scottish and Cornish subjects in the 1948 Exhibition.

The Annual Exhibition was carefully reviewed in the Chronicle of November 27th and it was noted that the work of the affiliated societies, the recently formed Skegness Club now among them, was hung without adjudication by the hanging committee. The Brannan family was singled out for special praise and their vigorous works had 'attracted much attention' as had the works of Miss Tyson, Miss Spence-Whyte and E. J. Worrall. Eric Hesketh Hubbard was the guest critic and he had an audience of 116. There is no record of his remarks, but as a landscape and architectural painter of great distinction he would no doubt have enjoyed the exhibition, part of which was shown in Gainsborough together with 100 local views by Karl Wood, the following January.

1948 A Brush with Abstraction – and High Praise

The LAS finally 'bit the bullet' and decided to have a Studio meeting about abstract and fantastic art on May 1st. Each member had to bring a non-representational painting or a study including distortion or unusual patterns. A very enjoyable evening was had by all.

B. Kirkland Jamieson RBA was in no doubt about the biggest LAS exhibition ever held. He told the Members that the show was exceptionally good, and that, as a critic, he liked it very much. Marchbank Salmon impressed with a large Cornish Fishing Village subject called 'Cornish Pattern', and E. J. Worrall's oil of Great

E.E. Brannan, *Cornfield 1952*

Coates Rectory was felt to be 'extremely strong and vigorous' while Kathleen Tyson's oil, 'By the Lower Ouse' was deemed impressive. Architect Stanley Barrell's winning design for a sign board for the local Red Cross was also on view, but the London headquarters preferred Cooper's design. There were some 'masterly examples of the Potter's art' by R. L. Blatherwick who was now teaching at Lincoln School of Art. Some 284 exhibits were shown by 126 members. Over 150 works were transferred to Cleethorpes for a highly praised exhibition in which each member of the Brannan family was singled out and Noel was even compared to van Gogh! A. E. Wade, the Principal of the Grimsby School of Art, was praised for his fine portraits, and Worrall, Tyson and Oyler were also mentioned. The headline in the Grimsby News ran: 'Brannan Family Shine at Artists' Exhibition'.

E.E Brannan, *Miss Naton's Cottage, Welbourn, Lincolnshire*

Francis Cooper on Sales

A troubling issue for the LAS had always been that of sales from the Exhibitions. This would continue for some years, and Cooper expressed his surprise that when visiting other shows of a lesser standard, he had noted more sales than in Lincoln. He also noted that these other shows had been in the summer months, and recommended that his theory should be tested by holding the 1949 Exhibition in August.

Duly held in August, the Annual Exhibition attracted over 8000 visitors, but Cooper must have been devastated to record only 6 sales – 3 fewer than the previous year. But the LAS was 'on a roll', and guest critic T. C. Dugdale RA, RP, declared that he had seen 'a lot of admirable work'.

Noel Brannan, *Bradbury Mill*

Peter Brannan, *Self Portrait*

Enter Tony Bartl

Antonin Bartl (1912-1998) had been invited by Marchbank Salmon to lecture in Fine Art in Lincoln. A Czechoslovakian, Bartl had trained in Prague, where he had briefly been taught by Oskar Kokosckha. A Communist, he became Head of Publicity for Twentieth Century Fox in Prague, during the 1930's, but during the Second World War he had been put in a Labour Camp, from which he had escaped to Vienna. In his Prague years he had painted his compatriot Hedy Lamarr, Clark Gable and all the big stars, but after the hardships of war he needed a period of recuperation and he came to England as a Visiting Artist with the Arts Council in 1947, re-training at Heatherley's School of Art under Iain

MacNab, since his qualifications were not recognised here, and he could not speak English. Marchbank Salmon was a friend of fellow Scot MacNab, and he first met Bartl at Heatherley's.

Bartl, a charming and charismatic man, made an immediate and lasting impact, and while the Echo reported Dugdale's praise for Tarttelin's negroid 'Baptism of Our Lord', ignoring Bartl, an unidentified news cutting carried a lengthy review which praised Bartl's 'Cornish Harbour' oil before all others. His eventual impact on the Society and on countless art students has become a Lincoln legend, with many current members acknowledging his influence.

Peter Brannan, *Cleethorpes Beach Scene*

Peter Brannan, *Still Life*

Meanwhile, with petrol for cars still scarce, attendance at several summer outings had not been high, but it is no great surprise that a proposed excursion to the Lincoln City Waterworks Estate at Elkesley had to be cancelled for lack of support.

A selection from the Annual Exhibition was shown in Grantham and was 'greatly appreciated'.

1950 'Pictures are painted for people's houses'

So thundered the art critic of the Sunday Times, Eric Newton, when he spoke at the Annual Exhibition in early November. 'A picture in an exhibition is in the wrong place,' he went on, and concluded on a note that must have sent the LAS home rejoicing:

'I implore the public to regard paintings not only as objects to admire but objects to acquire'.

Newton confessed himself to be rather bored by exhibitions, but said that in general the present one was 'extremely good', so good that he hoped the practical effect would be to persuade the public to buy for their homes.

The critic of the Chronicle waxed lyrical about the strong, boisterous and strident work of Worrall and Wade, and reckoned 'Worrall in oils and (E. E.) Brannan in watercolour' to be the chief representatives of the spirited exhibits on view. The Echo decided that a newcomer called Nikolai Kukso of Woodhall Spa was the

Tony Bartl, *Seascape*

star of the year with his 'magnificent portrait of his wife'. This Polish ex-serviceman was responsible for the marbling and countryside murals in the Kinema in the Woods at Woodhall Spa, and, like Carlos Sancha, another artist now exhibiting with the LAS; he had studio premises at Halstead Hall. Bartl was nowhere to be found in these reviews and was perhaps reserving his fire power for a major event…

…The 1951 Exhibition of Painting and Drawings at Foyle's Art Gallery, Charing Cross Road, London.

Only certain members of the Society were invited to exhibit in this exhibition, which was an exclusive showcase for the LAS. It took place during April and was

opened by the Society's President Captain Crookshank, who happened to be the MP for Gainsborough. 116 paintings and drawings were shown. Crookshank's speech is worth quoting:

'We welcome those who come to paint our great open spaces, our buildings and our churches. The Society, leavened as it is by a sprinkling of professional artists, can hold its own among the larger exhibitions in London. It has an air of confidence about its work and strikes out bravely into new ground.'

The Exhibition was visited by members of the Arts Council and favourably reviewed in the 'Art News

Tony Bartl, *John Piper*

Stanley Barrell, *Hill Top, Waddington, 1967*

Review'. It contained sculpture in stone and marble by Philip Pape of Barton-on-Humber, pots by Bob Blatherwick, and paintings by Bartl, Boden, Borrill, the Brannans, Clive Browne, G. W. Bailey, S. Bullock, C. W. Davis, Farrow, Spencer Ford, Garland, Kukso, the late W. J. Rayner, Malcolm Rivron, Marchbank-Salmon, Carlos and Sheila Sancha, Tyson, W. M. Smith, A. E. Wade, Cecil Hodgkinson, M. W. Holborow, Oyler, H. Robinson, Spence-Whyte, Henry Stanley, Eyre-Walker, Rosette Walker and Norman Wright.

The manager at Foyle's wrote that by general opinion the best picture had been Eyre Walker's 'The Cuillin', and that much praise had also gone to G. W. Bailey's 'Old Spalding', E. E. Brannan's 'Lincolnshire Dyke', and all of Garland's pictures. His own preference had been for E. E. Brannan and Judith Oyler.

An Equal Triumph – the 1951 Annual Exhibition

The success of LAS members in London, resulting in some being approached for reproduction rights, did not stop at Foyle's. A momentum was gathering, and in November the Annual Exhibition opened to the highest praise, with 232 exhibits, a call by the Opener, William Scott-Moncrieffe, for a Lincoln School of Art which would give its own diploma, and a remark by artist-critic Robert Melville about the watercolours being of a very high standard and continuing the traditions of the English Watercolour School. But even more pleasing to the Society was a suggestion by 'a special contributor' to the Echo, that at last, a true 'Lincoln School' of painters, on the model of similar schools in Norwich, St. Ives and Glasgow, had arrived. The contributor went on:

'This is a high claim, but Bartl, Brannan (all three of them), Worrall, Salmon, Byatt, Tyson are named among others in the catalogue that justify it... Some, however, Sancha and Eyre-Walker are conspicuous among them – have excellencies that cannot be said to derive from this particular...yet, being associated with this Society, they add lustre to it.'

Robert Melville praised in particular the work of the Brannans, and of Peter Brannan he said: 'No. 42 'Café Interior' by Peter Brannan is a beautiful rendering of an impression quickly seen and quickly stated, with such harmony of colour and arrangement that great names like Toulouse Lautrec and Victor Passmore come to mind.'

1952 'Worthy of London' – and a new Architectural Section

Patrick Ferguson Millard, the colourful principal of the Regent Street Polytechnic School of Art, and quite a pin-

Selection Committee at Work in the Usher Gallery, October 1948.
Standing: Mr. Batley; Mr. Smith; Mr. Eastcott; Mr. Farrow; Miss Smith (Keeper); Mr. Cooper (Hon. Secretary)
Seated: Mr. Bennett; Miss Spence-Whyte; Mr. Salmon; Miss Oyler; Mr. Wright; Mr. Bullock; Miss Tyson (Chairman)

up with the female students, continued the waves of recognition brought by 1951 when he told members at the Annual Criticism that they had a high standard of work worthy of exhibition in London and so superbly hung that many of London's galleries 'could with great advantage copy the Lincoln methods'. With civic openings now an established norm, the Society's profile in Lincoln itself was much higher, and in 1951 the idea was floated by Cooper that there might be a section in the Exhibition for architectural drawings and models. Architect Stanley Barrell was eventually asked to chair an

Architectural sub-committee and the result was indeed a new section in the 1952 Exhibition, with 29 entries. Cooper suggested that the Meeting following the Exhibition should have an architectural speaker of some eminence, and, as though a magic wand had been waved, Sir Hugh Casson duly arrived on November 29th to give a talk on 'Architecture and the Decorative Arts'. There was a large attendance. The new Architectural Section presented a fine opportunity for architects to show new projects like designs for schools, and restoration work on very old buildings, such as, in 1952, the work on the 'Cardinal's Hat' at the top of the High Street.

Studio Meetings and Meetings About the Studio

At this time, the studio sessions at the School of Art were thinly attended, and only 9 members came regularly. Cooper actually wondered whether the Society was 'really sociable', because the summer excursions 'had not raised much enthusiasm' either. Yet, in May 1951, Peter Scott visited Lincoln again, and at an informal gathering at Eastgate Court, 30 members heard him lecture on his Arctic travels. The Society's projected Studio was a real problem. Members objected strongly to some Corporation premises which had been found on Westgate, and in a survey, less than half the membership expressed themselves interested in the idea – which must have been a shock for the committee. The Studio Fund stood at £200, but the Westgate premises could only be occupied if an annual sum of £60 was raised by extra subscriptions. Perhaps the Members simply could not afford it. Full Membership averaged 53 at this time, with only a small proportion living in Lincoln itself.

1953 Keeping the Standard High

A sensible 218 exhibits, seven fewer than 1952, greeted Barnett Freedman CBE. RDI. at the Annual Exhibition in November. Comparing the work to exhibitions of other art societies and dealer-sponsored exhibitions in London, to the advantage of the LAS, he then delivered a first-rate criticism which pleased the members, and was 'as sharp in censure as he was in praise'. This encouraged the maintenance of high standards which could so easily fall if members allowed themselves to be lulled by what Cooper said had been the 'uniformly enthusiastic' comments of the 3,200 recorded visitors. 100 members exhibited, and a staggering 83 attended the criticism, which, compared with the 30 who went to Brocklesby Hall in July at Lord Yarborough's invitation, lends weight to Cooper's assertion that members were becoming exclusively focussed on the Exhibition.

1954

The Echo underlined the high status of the LAS when it declared: 'with a fine record in the art world, it is recognised as one of the foremost of provincial artists' societies in this country'.

But the Echo damaged the historical record by calling the original members of the 1906 Drawing Club a 'small handful' of enthusiastic Lincoln people. Nothing could have been further from the truth. 4069 visitors saw the Annual Exhibition in November, and 18 works sold- the highest number of sales ever. The critic was artist Edward Swann, who gave a searching criticism, and high praise for the overall standard. Swann went on to present a successful weekend drawing and painting course at Lincoln's Bishop's Palace in 1957, having been forced to cancel in 1955 because of the very poor response.

The Lincoln Society of Arts arranged a talk by Basil Spence OBE on 'Designing a Modern Cathedral' to which all members of the LAS were invited, on April 27th. Spence's original drawings of Coventry Cathedral were displayed and the event must have attracted the new architectural section members of the LAS.

1955 Another London Accolade

Selected Art Societies were invited to submit works for an exhibition at the Royal Institute in Piccadilly, during May, organised by the Workers' Travel Association. The LAS was one of them, and Edward Swann reappeared to make the selection at the Usher. 19 works were chosen from 12 members, and the LAS contributions looked very strong in the West Gallery of the Royal Institute.

Jack Merriott, R.I., was the critic for the autumn exhibition, and he praised the work and the hanging. He selected 15 paintings for their 'traditional or progressive attitudes of mind' and commented on each. The Chronicle described the exhibition of just over 200 items in terms that would have fitted the Society's exhibitions from its earliest years:

R.L. Blatherwick, *Thrown Pot*

'The exhibition shows Lincolnshire by road and river, by Cathedral and by haystack. Even its birds and flowers are on canvas. Exhibits include quite a lot of still life. Lincolnshire artists also ventured further afield and brought back glimpses of Venice, Corfu, Welsh glens and Cornish fishing villages.'

The press reported the death at 69 of George Boden, and recalled that he was a son of the founder of Boden's Ltd, the wholesale druggists of Lincoln. He died at his home in Elmley Castle, Worcestershire. Cooper wrote appreciatively that Boden's enthusiasm had been backed by much practical help, and that he had been a highly regarded member.

1956 Jubilee Year – A High-Water Mark – The President of the Royal Academy applauds the LAS

The Society's Jubilee Year was chiefly remarkable for the visit of Sir Albert Richardson the architect who succeeded Sir Gerald Kelly as P.R.A. in December 1954. This was an accolade, and Cooper recorded that he knew of no other Society similarly honoured, and that the visit was entirely the result of the Society's reputation.

The Annual Exhibition, preceded by a luncheon at the Saracen's Head Hotel at which Sir Albert was Guest of Honour, was well reviewed, and the Echo noted 'the very fine work' of A. K. Bartl, including his study for a mural for the British Welding Institute at Cambridge. Clive Browne, Worrall and Peter Brannan were next in line for praise, with Judith Oyler singled out in the women, and a watercolour of Steep Hill by Gilbert Farrow, Chairman at the time, was also praised. Monica Smith was pleased to see a painting of working life, which she reckoned was unique in the Society's history, by Neville Garton, an employee of Ruston's, depicting the Fuel Pump Shop at Anchor Street. Garton was an associate member.

Sir Alfred Speaks Out

As befits a President of the Royal Academy, Sir Albert delivered a tirade against 'metallic hypocrisy' in modern design, the desire for quick notoriety, rotten shops filled with unnecessary goods, and art critics incapable of drawing a line. He advised study of the Old Masters, and regular sketching, and the importance of taking time over the production of works. He praised the Architectural Section for the humanity in its designs, and noted the blues and greys around Lincoln which had influenced De Wint. Significantly, he suggested that the high standard of the exhibition was due entirely to the 'genus loci, of that wonderful architectural masterpiece, Lincoln Cathedral, equalled only by Durham.'

David Tarttelin, *Nativity - The Adoration Of The Shepherds*

News of his speech reached Sheffield and the Sheffield Telegraph ran a piece headlined 'Vigorous Art at Lincoln', while the Echo led with 'Artist lashes Out at the Luxurious, Vulgar, Bulbous'!

The Jubilee luncheon was not quite so turbulent, consisting of Cream Egyptienne, Poached Turbot, Roast Lamb, Gateau St. Honore, and Cheese and biscuits.

A guest critic had been invited in the person of R. O. Dunlop RA, who was unable to come at the last minute. The LAS invited him three times, and three times he was unable to come because of health problems. In 1957 Edward Swann gamely stepped into the breach with a few hours' notice.

The End of Affiliation

The year closed on a regretful note, for the affiliation of other Societies to the LAS was discontinued. For years, the four pieces of work which each full member was allowed to submit were only rejected if the size was deemed unwieldy, and the work of Associates was always subject to selection, but the affiliated Societies had their entries hung without any selection by the LAS committee, meaning that a lot of work was nowhere near the standard of most of the Exhibition. In time, with pressure on space mounting, this state of affairs became untenable. The press had noticed the discrepancies and had referred to them in a diplomatic way. The LAS acted decisively and were assured of the continuation of happy informal relations with the Boston, Grantham, North Lincs and Skegness Societies.

1957 E. E. Brannan Dies. Modesty and Greatness

Affectionate tributes were paid to Edward Eaton Brannan who died in May after thirty years of devotion to the LAS. The Echo acknowledged that 'but for his modesty' he would have achieved fame, and noted that he had exhibited at the Royal Academy, the Paris Salon and in many other prestigious places. He was 'in the great tradition of English Art', and his close relationship with Nature left no room for abstraction or 'isms'. He would, said the Echo, be long remembered. And so it has proved.

The press also mentioned during that year that Mrs. Mason and Miss King were the only two surviving original members. Both had served on the committee for many years. 'I'm not at all a shining light' said Miss King, echoing that modest spirit which imbued most of the Society's members. At the November AGM, Cooper noted with sadness the death of Mrs. Mason.

The Annual Exhibition comprised 185 works from 92 exhibitors and attracted 5000 visitors. There were 17 recorded sales, and an amazing 94 members attended Edward Swann's criticism, which was greatly appreciated for its 'acute remarks and lively manner'.

1958 Dunlop at Last

Judith Oyler succeeded Farrow as Chairman while Worrall announced he could not accept any position on the committee since he would be shortly leaving the district. He retired to the South Coast.

At the fourth attempt the LAS succeeded in getting R.O. Dunlop RA to deliver the criticism at the Annual Exhibition, and despite his continuing illness he said how very much he had been looking forward to coming. He 'neither spared nor scourged' and found much to praise, concluding that the exhibition was good enough for Bond Street. Part of the exhibition was afterwards shown in Newark.

H. M. Sutton begs to differ...

A salutary view of the Exhibition was given in a specially written review in the Echo by H M Sutton, the Principal of Mansfield School of Art. Headlined 'A Packet of All Sorts', the article had several major points:

'With amateurs exhibiting alongside professionals, real problems confront selection committees. 'Must their (the amateurs') every effort be hung in places reserved for works of art?'

Most members *'are content to look at the same sort of thing in much the same sort of way.'*

'The play of imagination is rare.'

'I found too little creative art in this large exhibition.'

However, Sutton praised unreservedly the works of Peter Brannan 'with (their) fine streak of individual vision', and noted that his brother Noel had 'vigour but less individuality'. But Miss Tyson's 'Sampans in Hong Kong Harbour' 'had too many boats forced into a curving pattern'.

'Two large limping horrors' are not attributed, and the work of new member Mrs. Patricia Laing was deemed *'a successful piece of realism'*.

Overall, this article would give members a lot of food for thought, but it will be noted that Peter Brannan continued to pass all tests. His star was ascending.

1959 Lessons are learned as the decade closes

Patricia Laing was from the start a devoted member and was soon put onto the committee. With the committee's authority she told the Echo that for the 1959 Exhibition, 'Quality rather than quantity' was the watchword. The number of paintings exhibited by associates dropped dramatically by 24, to 54, as a result of the committee's decision to raise the standard. Sutton's warnings had been heeded. Leonard Richmond RBA ROI, the St. Ives artist, distinguished landscapist and author of books on painting, gave a brief criticism which Cooper found 'highly complimentary, incisive and of great value'.

Kenneth Long RBA ATD, Deputy Principal of Nottingham School of Art, followed in his colleague Sutton's footsteps to write for the Echo. This time, closing the LAS's most exciting decade on a high and healthy note, he said that there were many works in the exhibition of great sensitivity and excellence, and again praised Peter Brannan:

> *'Clearly, Mr. Brannan has an accurate eye but he is also most concerned that what he represents never interferes with or subdues his enjoyment of paint and the formal geometry and order of his Mondrian-like designs.'*

Marchbank Salmon and Patricia Laing were also praised for their sensitivity to design and skilful paintwork. Long detected a secondary category of painters, 'painting what they feel' about their subjects, and cited Bartl, Zakrzewski, Worrall, T. Hiley and K. Hoult as representatives of this school.

Sir Charles Tennyson had opened the exhibition on October 24th. Miss King was still exhibiting her rose pictures, and was now the Society's auditor. After 53 years the town of Mansfield received the benefit of 58 works from the exhibition in a New Year show until January 30th 1960.

A Joker in the Pack

Richard Duffill, an Associate non-artist, played an effective joke on the Society by exhibiting an accidentally-made imprint of an over inked stencil cut by someone in his office. The hanging committee accepted it, perhaps nervously anxious to present some abstract work – but it appears to have been a very poor piece, and according to the Echo who told the story, Leonard Richmond ignored it – very wisely!

5

New Ventures in the Swinging 'Sixties

David Hollinshead, *Two Trees*

David Paton, *Rainbow, Ardnamurchan*

The most significant development in the 1960's was the introduction of Spring Exhibitions of Prints, Drawings and Watercolours at the Usher, an idea of Peter Brannan's which was designed to emphasise the professionalism and range of Members' work and enhance the stature of the county's leading Art Society. Also, from 1965, the LAS organised touring exhibitions with the newly formed Lincolnshire Association, and Abstract Art gained a temporary foothold.

1960 Cooper says Farewell

With the retirement of Francis Cooper to Southwold in Suffolk, and the death of Viscount Crookshank in 1961, the Society lost two outstanding organisers. Crookshank, as the leader of the House of Commons, had known many of the top people in London, attracting them to Lincoln to open the Society's exhibitions. Trenchard Cox CBE was a case in point. Director of the Victoria and Albert Museum, he opened the 1960 Exhibition, while another key player on the move, Marchbank Salmon, was invited to give the Criticism. He went on to Croydon School of Art and his successor as Principal of the Lincoln School of Art was the young and innovative Kenneth Gribble, who was welcomed onto the committee on October 8th. E. J. Worrall, who had retired to Steyning in Sussex in 1959, continued to show work in Lincoln in 1960, but his increasing back problems and distance from Lincoln no doubt obliged him to terminate his membership. He had been an inspirational figure, and had helped many of his pupils at Wintringham to get into the Slade.

Cooper's Legacy

New Chairman Stanley Barrell, succeeding Judith Oyler, told the November AGM that the prestige now accruing to the Society was the result of Francis Cooper's leadership and inspiration since he joined in 1937. Cooper replied that he had received many kindnesses and spoke of the joy of being Honorary Secretary, inscribing a moving message in the minutes:

"Very best of good wishes for the Society's future, and thanks for good comradeship."

Francis Cooper November 3rd 1960.

He kept in touch with Gribble, and wrote from Southwold to say how much he missed his work. He had brought national recognition to the Society and he never forgot those who had helped in the cause, especially Monica Smith. Significantly, he continued to paint and exhibit in Southwold.

Issues of Adjudication

A Special Committee Meeting on November 20th 1960 discussed increasing unease in the membership about the submissions of Full Members not being subject to adjudication by the hanging committee. Oyler, always protective of Full Members' privileges, may well have influenced the outcome, which was that adjudication was still not necessary providing that more stringent standards were applied to the election of Full Members.

This was put to the Members at the October AGM in 1961. It was decided that Full Members would be adjudicated, and this was made official policy in the December meeting. Thus, the concerns of many Associates began to be addressed, but it would be decades before a decisive and satisfactory solution could be found.

The 1960 Annual Exhibition

Trenchard Cox underlined the standing of the LAS in his Opening speech, saying he was struck by the very high standard. He continued: "It is a great pleasure to see an exhibition with such variety and such interest as this," and commented that one sees so many which have only one especial quality. In the preceding Criticism, Marchbank Salmon gave a bouquet to the Society by saying that in the 14 years he had been associated with the exhibitions, there had been an enormous improvement in standard.

Geoffrey Wilson, *Framlingham Castle*

The committee meeting of October 8th, prior to the Exhibition, had welcomed Lincoln's latest City Architect R. R. Alexander as a Member, and had nominated Kenneth Gribble as Honorary Secretary.

An Abstract Interlude

The Society continued its flirtation with Abstraction when guest speaker Frank Avray-Wilson delivered a talk on the principles of his abstract paintings on November 26th.

The audience of 100 were told that "if you paint nature – which I once did very badly – the odds are that the vitalism in nature will be reduced unless you are a very great painter. With abstract painting, it is possible to create a form of life stronger than would be found in any situation in nature." Numerous questions were asked, which is hardly surprising for a Society which clearly still painted traditionally.

Geoffrey Wilson, *Tangiers From The East*

1961 Enter Tom Baker

On May 6th Chairman Stanley Barrell proposed that Tom Baker, the new Director of Museums, Art Gallery and Libraries, be elected as an honorary member. Baker was a very popular figure who would soon become Treasurer and Secretary of the Society, but in 1961 Gribble proposed that from then on the Treasurer should be a different person from the Secretary because the Secretary's work had grown. Initially therefore, with Gribble as Secretary, Tom Baker became Treasurer and Membership Secretary. Lord Crookshank died, and warm tributes were paid about his dedication to the Society, but his successor, the Earl of Ancaster, proved to be an equally dedicated, 'hands-on' President, who even helped to prepare rooms for meetings, and attended as many as he could, writing his distinctive letters in green ink and taking a personal interest in members which was long remembered and appreciated.

Geoffrey Wilson, *Low Meadows, Mettingham*

To Louth and Barton-on-Humber

In June, the Society visited Louth for a sketching day, this being the first time it had been to Louth for this purpose. Jack Yates (John Betjeman's great friend and sometime member of the British Council, whose father had been Vicar of St. Michael's in Louth) wrote to Gribble extolling his home town:

"You see, I don't know what your people like to do. They might like to try the architectural features (the church) which many thousands have tried before – even the younger Pugin was not wildly successful. Or some may have the tastes of a friend of mine who never stops painting grain elevators in Canada."

There was also a successful visit to the historic Tyrwhitt Hall at Barton on Humber, at the invitation of the Papes. The sculptor Philip Pape had exhibited with the LAS for several years.

On October 23rd, Colin Dudley, Principal of the Intermediate School of Painting at Loughborough College of Art, told Society members at their Annual Usher Exhibition that there were 'some very distinguished paintings, and there is no bad work.'

'Still Too Lenient'

Notwithstanding Dudley's enthusiasm, Peter Brannan sent a letter to the Committee in late November, saying that he considered the policy of the Selection Committee 'still too lenient', and proposing a Spring exhibition of Drawing in one of the Usher's smaller galleries. The idea was warmly received.

Mrs. Jane Kennedy, Noel Brannan's daughter, recalled that the family was very much against the idea of the LAS as a society where 'Sunday painters' could exhibit. Gribble echoed this when he told Mrs. Birkett and Miss King that 'no-one has the right to exhibit after having had four lessons or painting four pictures.' The ladies had tried to propose that associate members might have one work exhibited without selection. It was a nice try!

After the AGM, the colourful Lincoln architect Sam Scorer gave a lecture on 'Town Planning and Lincoln.' He would exhibit frequently with the LAS as a painter as well as an architect.

1962 Gribble and Grimble

With John Grimble, the Boston art teacher and sculptor in the Chair, and his near-namesake Gribble as Secretary, the LAS entered a period of pleasant confusion. Letters prove that the two men got on well and in one of these Grimble said how he could appreciate the feeling amongst some associate members that the selection committee was a 'closed shop', choosing the same sort of work by the same people year after year. But the Society continued to vary its activities and in February there was a screening of films about Picasso, Braque and Jackson Pollock, which were warmly received. Then came the first Spring

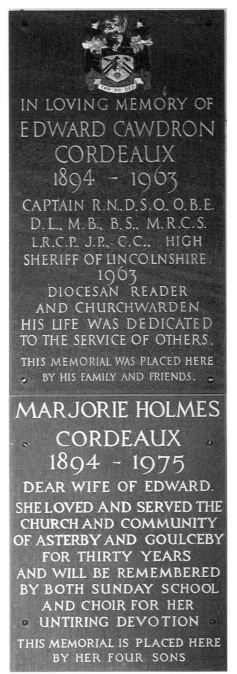

Philip Pape, *Inscription*

Patricia Laing, *Cornish Fishing Boat*

Exhibition of Prints and Drawings, opened on March 10th at the Usher, and greeted as a great success, with three sales. Gribble's Annual Report states that the Society realised the importance of this event as a demonstration of the high standards it needed to display as the County's leading art society. It was unanimously agreed that the Spring Exhibition should be repeated in 1963.

Howard Shelton recommends…

The LAS was grateful to critic Howard Shelton, Principal of Hornsey College of Art, for an excellent criticism of the 1962 Annual Exhibition during which he recommended that 'the Society should begin painting pictures of the City and County as they are now, for the future record, and money should be put aside to buy these paintings for the Usher.' Images of historic Lincoln had abounded in the exhibitions and Shelton's call was clearly aimed at a more comprehensive contemporary visual survey of Lincolnshire capturing more than just the usual 'beauty spots'. He concluded that the exhibition was 'one of the better exhibitions' he had seen of provincial societies. 125 items from 59 exhibitors were displayed, indicating far more rigour in the selection process.

Although Farrow, Oyler and Brough retired from the committee 'with the Society's gratitude', a new Society member, Nottinghamshire-born David Paton, who trained at Lincoln School of Art and became Head of Ceramics and 3D Design at Grimsby, was elected on November 24th. He would become something of a father figure to the LAS, and encourage other talents to join. On the same day Colin Anson presented a lecture on Venetian Painting, and the AGM heard a call for an exhibition of rejects and Associates' work. The Committee 'agreed to consider the matter,' but nothing was done.

1963 People in Snow

The second Spring Exhibition of Prints and Drawings was opened on March 1st and attracted just under 3000 visitors. One work was sold, Peter Brannan's 'People in Snow' which Gribble found most suitable, given the significant winter snowfall that year! Perhaps the snow hindered the progress of members' various art projects, for at the Annual Exhibition only 107 exhibits (by 56 Members) were shown, and several of these were by new members making their debut, some a year ahead of their election as Full Members. These included Christopher Brighton, part-time lecturer at the Lincoln School of Art, whose innovative work impressed the forward-looking Gribble and received favourable mention in the Echo, 'catching the eye with their bold execution.' They were both abstracts with enticing titles – 'Painting on a Dramatic Theme', and 'The Birth of Venus'. Other new exhibitors were David Paton with two of his signature landscapes, and David Hollinshead who contributed an abstract landscape 'Risegate Eau'. The

two Brannans made a strong showing and Bartl was singled out for his portrait of his wife Sheila. Miss Dudding dug herself in to a 'Cornfield at Winteringham' while Oyler had clearly been in Scotland, at Kirkcudbright. I. Houston A.R.C.M. caught both snow and sun with 'Snow at Cherry Willingham' and 'Summer Storm Near Branston' but there were a few titles indicative of the contemporary country-wide survey recommended by Howard Shelton including T.H. White's 'Immingham Dock' and R. R. Alexander's 'Burton Lane End near Lincoln'. Dudding's 'Humber at Winteringham' was, characteristically, not for sale. Grimble, Blatherwick and Clarke provided five items of sculpture and pottery.

There was, for the first time in many years, no invited critic, but Lord Ancaster invited 164 members and their guests to accept his hospitality at the Opening – a most generous gesture.

The Echo concluded that the 1963 Exhibition had 'a variety and richness well worth seeing'. Certainly there had been a refreshing emphasis on Abstraction, with Hugh Robinson of the Lincoln School of Art and Pat Laing joining Chris Brighton with several other abstract compositions in the 'non-figurative' section. Abstraction had arrived.

1964 Decidedly anti-social

The summer outings had not been well attended for some time, so the committee, now under the Chairmanship of R.R. Alexander, sent out a questionnaire. Replies were considered on April 19th. From a membership of 220, thirty replied and five of those indicated no interest in the outings. The most comical understatement in the history of the Society's minutes occurred when Gribble recorded that 'this showed that the majority of members were not interested.' Sadly, the Papes had to be informed that their latest kind offer of hospitality at Tyrwhitt Hall must be turned down, and it was decided that the matter of summer outings would be dropped 'for this year'.

R. R. Alexander then requested the committee to rise in memory of the late Canon Arthur Cook 'whose presence had always enlivened the society's functions'. Canon Cook also wrote memorably about his beloved Lincoln Cathedral.

There was a call for a third kind of annual exhibition, of watercolours and gouache paintings, which was eventually accommodated by titling the Spring exhibition 'Prints, Drawings and Watercolours'.

A Good Year for New Members

Several associate members were elected to Full Membership. Mrs. Alison Wilson and Mrs. J. Oakley joined Messrs. F. V. A. Wells, I. M. Houston, David Hollinshead and Christopher Brighton. Messrs. P. Morwood, M. Simpson, John Foster and Ken Lee were also made Full Members.

Ken Lee, the new Lecturer in Painting in Lincoln was invited to present the Annual lecture. Appointed by Gribble along with John Foster as Senior Lecturer, they replaced Bartl, whose justifiable distress resonated with many sympathetic friends. Lee had not knowingly supplanted Bartl, however, and the two men got on well. Lee had always been a very highly regarded member and, like Bartl, he enjoyed working on a large scale, but felt equally at home in watercolours. For his November lecture to the Society he spoke about the creative process, and worked on an abstract painting.

The Spring Exhibition took place from 1st-31st May and was held in the newly decorated Curtois Wing of the Usher. The show was seen by 5,146 visitors.

Unusual Titles

The Annual Exhibition was opened by the Mayor of Lincoln, Councillor Woolhouse, on October 24th. Gribble recorded that this opening, with its Civic Party, was 'a return to the more formal ways of earlier years.' 151 works were hung out of 237 received, and 65 members were represented. Pat Laing showed two oils of her favourite painting area at Blakeney in North Norfolk.

Oyler and Dudding had clearly been to the Mendips and Peter Brannan decided that yet another snow scene was called for after his last one had been the only picture sold in the 1963 Spring Show. Brighton served up 'Off Balance', and T. H. Gregson presented 'Island of Discontent'. Mr. A. Saunders the Principal of Chesterfield College of Art, gave the criticism which Gribble felt was 'stimulating and well considered'.

1965 A letter from a very old Member

Gribble may have been pleased with the 'return to more formal ways' at the Openings of the Exhibitions, but Ralph Sharpe, who had joined in 1920, was not. In a withering attack on the Society contained in a letter of 18th November, he said:

> 'The Society is not so jolly, friendly and carefree as it was about 40 years ago in the days of Mr. Garland, Mr. Storey and Mr. Boden. It's getting too officious, there's too much pomposity and snobbery'.

His 1965 entry, on a medieval literary theme, was rejected, so his indignation might be expected. But he thundered on about the absence of craftsmanship, and urged one exhibition for the moderns and one for the traditionalists. In effect, the LAS had already achieved this at the Usher, and particularly in 1965, when Gribble noted how gratifying it was 'to have achieved one room of contemporary material'. This material included two 'constructions' by Brighton which Gribble hailed as 'the artist's quest for self-expression, an experimental approach to interplay of timber surfaces, and, one may add, adhesives'. Gribble even-handedly praised Lee and Bartl, Brannan and Laing. The Autumn Exhibition was opened by Dick Taverne, the Lincoln MP, who grabbed the headlines with his support for an Arts Centre for Lincoln, and the criticism was given by Kenneth Long ARCA of Loughborough College of Art, whose remarks were 'very appreciative and most helpful'.

Finally for 1965, the Spring Exhibition, opened by Capt. Jeremy Elwes of the Lincolnshire Association, had attracted 3,751 visitors, and 10 pictures were sold.

John Grimble, *Boston Skyline*

Hugh Robinson, *Untitled*

On Tour with the Lincolnshire Association

John Betjeman, in his speech at the Inauguration of the Lincolnshire Association in 1965 had expressed a desire to see Lincolnshire with its own flag and needing passports to get in. The object of the Association was to foster and promote artistic taste and knowledge, and the understanding and appreciation of the arts and heritage of the county. Kenneth Gribble, in 1965 the Chairman of the Visual Arts Panel of the new Association, wanted the LAS to wave its own flag and undertake once again a touring exhibition to several centres within the county. 40 works were chosen from the Annual Exhibition and,

under the auspices of the Lincolnshire Association, they formed the first exhibition at Lord Ancaster's new Willoughby Memorial Gallery at Corby Glen, erected in memory of his son Lord Timothy Willoughby. Other venues were Grimsby, Barton-on-Humber, Boston, Grantham and Gainsborough.

Enter Geoffrey Wilson

Proposed by Mr. K. Hoult, Norfolk-born Geoffrey Wilson, a chartered land agent for Sir Edmund Bacon's estates near Gainsborough, was elected a Member. Wilson knew and admired Arnesby Brown and had been encouraged to paint by Anna Airy. He had also been influenced by Rollett, Roland Fisher of Yarmouth and Dr. Pilcher. A very affable man, he threw himself into the life of the LAS with gusto and was soon inviting members out to Thonock Park for a sketching day. Eventually he became Chairman – on two occasions – and President. Ironically, he provided the solution to Mr. Sharpe's problem over the LAS being 'less jolly'. Under Geoffrey Wilson, the LAS even became 'social' again. But that story will unfold in its proper place…

1966

'The cathedral clock having struck seven, the meeting was declared open and the Chairman Mrs. Brough spoke a personal tribute to the memory of the late Gilbert Farrow, who was a most liked member of the Society for 22 years, eleven of which were as a member of this committee and was chairman in the Society's fiftieth year. He will be missed as a friend…members rose in silence in memory of a beloved member.' (Committee Meeting, July 5th).

1966 would be Gribble's last year as secretary and in his final Annual Report he records the Society's indebtedness to the Usher, without which it would 'not be able to continue in these days of high costs without heavily increased subscriptions or hanging fees'. But it had been a good year to end his seven years as secretary, for the Spring Exhibition sold work totalling £252.5.6d and the Annual Exhibition had realised 19 sales. 153 works were hung, by 75 artists, and the critic was Peter Lewis, Gregory Fellow of Fine Art, Nottingham University. Some idea of the difficulties the selection committee had to face – and continue to face – is given by the fact that 272 works were submitted by 119 artists, meaning that 44 artists experienced disappointment or worse. Perhaps the Public lecture which closed the exhibition diverted members, for it was a talk on polymer colours by Charles Pierce of Messrs. Reeves. The unusual selection of works from the Exhibition then went on tour yet again under the auspices of the Lincolnshire Association. Earlier in the year, on June 11th, the sketching outing to Gainsborough received the hospitality of Geoffrey Wilson and his wife, and Mrs. Doris Hartley, a fine portraitist and colourist, organised this and several other events at this time. Like so many other members, she had trained at the Lincoln School of Art, but was unique in choosing to exhibit her clay figure-models.

1967 Big Changes and a Shock Decision

Kenneth Gribble left Lincoln in April to become Principal of the Taunton College of Art. Margaret Brough presented him with a cheque from members and thanked him for his great interest in, and work for, the Society. He then opened the Spring Exhibition of Drawings, Watercolours and Prints, which ran from March 18th to April 22nd. By September 30th, Tom Baker had become secretary – quite a commitment when he was originally invited into the Society simply for the pleasure of his company! The new Principal of the School of Art, Arthur W. H. Pears, opened the Annual Exhibition on October 21st. In his speech he referred to the new School of Art he was involved in planning, and said he wanted to see the end of the terms 'amateur' and 'professional' in the art world. The LAS had, he felt, already achieved this, and the show was 'the most exciting exhibition I have seen by an artists' society'. The euphoria of this speech had, by all accounts, already been extinguished by the guest critic, David Carr-Smith Dip. R. A., a part-time lecturer in painting in Sheffield. It had been Gribble's idea to invite him.

On the Edge of a Volcano

Mrs Brough was already worried about Carr-Smith earlier in October when she wrote to the Society's temporary secretary, John Foster. The letter is worth quoting in length:

'I must confess I'm a bit alarmed at the thought of a critic who spends so much time thinking about painting that he hasn't any time to paint…I had no

idea we rejected all Mary Dudding's work this year. What a calamity! I know what she wants the committee names for. She will go round the exhibition and count the pictures hung of every member of the committee, and then will see them off at the A.G.M....Miss Oyler...I believe we rejected some of hers...she merely commented on the fact that a lot of people were going to be disappointed this year...you'll get the brickbats from Miss Dudding, I expect...Mr. Gribble had a wonderful barbed politeness for dealing with these matters from the platform, a sort of icy gracefulness that left his assailants speechless...let's hope it won't come to a fight'.

Older members, who remember the occasion, but not the name of Carr-Smith, agree on the devastating effect he had. Beginning quietly, he then ripped off his tie, and laid into the works on view, saying that they had nothing whatever to do with painting. At the end, everyone felt demoralised and destroyed. Miss Dudding was, in the event, well out of it. No record exists in the minutes of any of this, and the ultimate irony was that Gribble had been questioning the need for guest critics, but had been howled down by members who felt they had a valuable function. Perhaps Pears decided to tell them it had been a most exciting exhibition in order to restore morale. But the decision to hang only 142 works, 41 of which were by Associates, sounds rigorous and fair. Bartl, Hollinshead, Peter Brannan and Geoffrey Wilson appear to have made a strong showing and were joined by Francis Le Marchant whose continental panoramas were becoming a very polished feature of the shows. Laing, Oyler, Hartley and Cartwright batted for the women while the usual woodcarvings by Grimble and ceramics by Bob Blatherwick were joined by P. Morwood, Miss B. E. Hunt and Mrs. D. Smith all showing their pots. The firms of Anthony Parker and John Roberts showed their latest architectural contributions to Lincolnshire.

Earlier in the year the committee had heard repeated protests from associates and a call for a 'Salon des Refuses', but Mrs. Brough stated that since the committee were in agreement over the standard of rejected works there was no need for the committee to take any action over them. She could be quite formidable, and her view prevailed.

1968 Beauty Around Us – but how much?

The Spring Exhibition was re-titled 'Drawings, Prints and Transparent Watercolours' after members had submitted some paintings employing dense media. 93 works from 38 members and associates realised a total of 11 sales. Between February and December the travelling exhibition was seen in Grantham, Caistor, Gainsborough, Boston, Scunthorpe, Corby Glen, Lincoln (Bishop Grosseteste College), Spilsby and Tyrwhitt Hall, Barton-on-Humber. There were, surprisingly, no sales from this extensive venture, although Councillor Mrs. P. M. West of Louth was a patron of the Society at this time.

On October 19th the Echo carried a large photograph of J. A. M. Aldridge, RA, the critic for the Annual Exhibition, holding forth before members. The Echo's 'Gossiper' wrote on Oct 22nd: 'Methinks Aldridge was being either jocular or cynical when he told members that by their work, they had paid tribute to what little beauty is left around us.' Gossiper cautioned that 'We haven't reached 1984 yet. There is still a great deal that is beautiful to look at.'

Aldridge was from Great Bardfield in Essex, and was being promoted by Tom Baker, (now Secretary after John Foster's brief interim contribution) as a representative of East Anglian artists. His rather dark assessment remains an enigma but the records state that his visit was very much appreciated. In a similar situation to the previous year, 149 works were selected from the 235 submitted, and 69 out of 99 members had their work accepted, with 18 sales.

1969 The Architectural Section is disbanded

In 1963 the exhibits of the Architectural Section were numerous and 5 exhibitors were given a central space in the second gallery at the Usher. In 1965 there had been 13 architectural exhibits, but in 1968 these had dwindled to 5 and they were not displayed as part of the overall exhibition. On April 11th 1969 Tom Baker wrote to the architects to say that the committee felt the section had not been as successful as hoped and had not served the purpose for which it was originally intended, so it had been decided to discontinue the idea. It was hoped the architects would remain as Members and exhibit alongside other Members, and this did happen. The Chairman at the time was Stanley Barrell, the original Chair of the Architectural sub-committee in 1952, and he went on to show many architectural watercolours, particularly of Italian buildings. Sam Scorer also made several notable contributions, as did R. W. Clarke of Sleaford.

Yet Another new fashion for Spring

Once again, the Spring exhibition changed its title, this time to 'Prints and Monochrome Drawings.' Oyler insisted on monochrome working drawings when Gribble had urged members to show more in the way of truly preparatory work, and this would lead to a clash in 1970, but it seems that the original intention of the exhibition was being subverted with watercolours and gouaches. The decade was drawing to a close, but the problems over the contents of the Spring Exhibition went on into the Seventies.

A Famous Artist-Critic

It so happened that Edward Bawden CBE, RA, had family connections in Lincoln, and when he and his wife came to pass comment on the Autumn Exhibition, opened on October 25th, they stayed in Canwick with her brother William Epton. Bawden, famous as an illustrator, was the subject of one of the Penguin monographs on 'Modern Painters'. The Echo reported that he found the standard at the LAS *'remarkably good'* and that he had seen a *'considerable variety of work with some excellent paintings.'* By contrast, his speech was remembered as rambling, over-long, and incoherent. No matter. The Society had attracted a big name and the decade closed with a flourish.

6

The Battle for Quality 1970-1979

David Morris, *Teapot*

David Morris, *Tuscan Snow*

Alma Paget, *Culverthorpe*

1970 Williams, Wood and Wilson

A young man called Peter Williams had succeeded Pears as Principal of Lincoln College of Art at Easter, and another young man, Richard Wood, had succeeded Monica Smith as the Keeper of the Usher. Apart from giving an LAS lecture on Industrial Design, Pears had not involved himself with the Society to anything like the extent of his predecessors, and Tom Baker wrote a letter to Peter Williams on August 17th inviting him to become Secretary and Treasurer.

'We should like to see the LAS come back into the orbit of the College of Art' said Baker, adding that he saw the LAS as an important link between the Usher and the wider Lincolnshire Community. He felt the Society had become *'heavily dependent on him'* to keep going, and had a 'declining membership' at the time, although the recorded figure for 1969, showing 59 Full Members and 156 Associates, would hardly suggest this. Baker was no doubt referring to the small number of Members who took a really active interest in the Society. Some, including the 1970 Chairman Mrs. Iona Cartwright, found

Lucy Marschner, *British Alpine Goat*

it difficult to travel from Boston for meetings, and her apologies are on record on several occasions. She was a very accomplished animal painter, and horses were her speciality.

Richard Wood willingly became the assistant secretary and treasurer and worked very closely with Williams, placing the entire facilities of the Usher at the service of the Society. Williams recalls that they worked towards modernising the exhibitions by encouraging subjects other than the *'interminable flat Lincolnshire landscapes that tended to dominate every show,'* and to insist on quality even if every work submitted by a full member had to be turned down.

Geoffrey Wilson deputised for Mrs. Cartwright and succeeded her as Chairman, but his first two-year stint in the job radiated enthusiasm and amiability and he showed a firm hand in meetings, creating the impression

that he was Chairman for a much longer period. Clearly his influence was still felt when he became 'immediate past Chairman', with the architect R. W. Clark succeeding him.

Williams, Wood and Wilson guided the LAS for the entire decade and were helped by a woman who has since become a Society legend, and who joined in 1970 – Gill Nadin.

Enter Gill Nadin

Taught at Bath Academy of Art by William Scott, Gill Nadin then studied in London, taught art in Bedford, married, had children and moved to Louth where she had relatives. She was in her early '40's when she became a member of the LAS and within 6 years she was its Chairman. Her strong personality and devotion to art was a match for Judith Oyler, but she became a great teacher and inspired many to have more confidence in their abilities. Eventually she joined the staff of Lincoln College of Art and inspired her students to join the LAS. Never tight or formulaic, her work radiated spontaneity and she was in the vanguard of the many women Members of the 1980's who refreshed and reinvigorated the appearance of the Exhibitions. Appropriately, she became Exhibitions Secretary in the 1980's.

Autumn Events Streamlined, and the Art College Link Restored

For some time, Members had been reluctant to travel twice to Lincoln for the Opening of the Annual Exhibition and the AGM at its conclusion. Most of the Annual Reports had read: 'the Exhibition now closing was seen by…' but the same paragraph could never give a final tally of visitor numbers or total sales. The committee decided to hold the AGM on the same day as the Opening, a practice which seems to have held to the present day.

At the 1970 AGM, Williams spoke about the facilities that would be available for Society meetings at the College of Art, and a December 4th meeting was agreed at the College to finalise arrangements subject to the feelings of

Max Marschner, *Packet (Screenprint)*

the Members. As a result there were Workshop Evenings at 7.00pm each Friday in winter, well attended by an average of 25 members.

Support from Bishop Grosseteste College

At this time, Camberwell-trained Max Marschner, a printmaker and lecturer at Bishop Grosseteste College in Lincoln, became a member along with his colleagues Ian Fraser and Denis Valentine. Valentine, a Leicester-trained

painter, later had a gallery in Navenby where the committee occasionally met. They were in the vanguard of lecturers who would eventually be attracted into the Society by Williams, and they believed that art should have strong links with the community. Max would become Chairman in 1979 while his wife Jill and daughter Lucy, also artists, would exhibit frequently and become the LAS's exhibiting family.

Ian Fraser, *Noah's Ark (Linocut)*

Dennis Valentine, *Rocks and Sand*

An American Exchange

1970 marked the 350th Anniversary of America's 'home town', Plymouth Massachusetts. The Pilgrim Fathers had set out from Boston in 1620 on their famous voyage to N. America, and as part of Plymouth Massachusetts' Annual Outdoor Art Show, works by artists from 'the Lincolnshire Artists' Association of Lincolnshire County, England', were to be shown in historic Brewster Gardens, laid out in 1620, while the work of 13 award-winning Massachusetts artists were to be sent to Lincoln and displayed in the Curtois wing of the Usher. Geoffrey Wilson and the munificent Gainsborough patron Mr. Herbert Whitton were instrumental in enabling the project to proceed, and this first American appearance by the LAS was a feather in the Society's cap. Grimble sent a woodcarving and an appropriate oil of Boston Stump; while Wilson sent Lincoln and east coast scenes, also in oil, and Barrell sent some landscapes as did Charles

Joan Lock, *Conservatory With Japanese Poster (Linocut)*

Harold Gosney, *Summerhouse*

Whitaker. Ian Fraser sent watercolours of 'Cornish stone', 'Serpentine Stone' and 'Quartz Pebble'. Oddly, these were described as pastels in the American catalogue!

With only five male members sending work, the exhibits did not reflect the overall membership of the LAS and the minutes reveal disappointment from some quarters that their work was not accepted, but the exhibits were carefully chosen for their historical appropriateness. The Exchange took place in September.

Avril Morris, *Green Jug*

The Spring Exhibition from March 26th – April 26th, was entitled 'Prints and Monochrome Drawings' and contained two works by David Paton intended as ironic comments on his skirmish with Oyler about her insistence on monochrome working drawings after he had first submitted a coloured one. 'Carte Blanche' and 'Bone Idle' explored issues argued over in committee regarding the coloured drawings and the hinterland between title and product.

The Annual Exhibition opened on October 24th with Williams as guest critic, had 152 exhibits including sculpture from four people. J. Instone's 'Predator IV' and 'Vertibrate II' joined three carvings by Grimble, a terra-cotta head by Margaret Clarke, and J. Jones's 'Plant Forms'. Charles Speed showed a 'doomed church' at Gayton-le-Marsh, while all the usual exhibitors were featured, and Oyler contributed her Isle of Mull watercolours, reserving her Mull drawings for the next Spring Exhibition. Ian Fraser showed 'Assisi', 'Florence' and 'Red Stone', while four Peter Brannan's were 'not for sale'.

1971 Art in a Postal Strike

Peter Williams recalls that Lincoln was in some turmoil at this time, with heavy industry in rapid decline, a high level of unemployment, social pessimism, and a lengthy postal strike. The strike disrupted arrangements for the Spring Exhibition, 'Prints and Monochrome Drawings', and Williams wrote to Members to say that they could therefore submit up to six works this year (Associates up to three!) in order to counter the poor response. The committee ruled that 'Drawings in which emphasis is upon colour masses rather than line were not acceptable'. 73 works were selected, 5000 visitors saw the exhibition, and Hugh Robinson showed five drawings, so his six submissions (if he indeed submitted six) were worthwhile.

The Autumn Exhibition

This carried an alphabetically arranged catalogue with no separate section for sculpture and ceramics, but Mrs. D. Smith exhibited wall plaques, Bob Blatherwick had the usual four pots, and Grimble showed four sculptures. Tony Bartl was notably absent, but no doubt preparing for a separate Usher exhibition of his works in 1973. The Brannans were out in force, Noel showing those industrial Leicestershire subjects which became a hallmark, and Oyler continued to offer the Isle of Mull. Max and Jill Marschner, David Morris and Paton made a strong showing. The Opener Critic for this November 6th – December 5th exhibition was Michael Gough, Chairman of the Society of Designer-Craftsmen.

Keith Roper, *Saltmarsh*

An Appeal to the County's other Art Societies

The Committee felt it was necessary to increase and broaden the membership and in the process to rectify the Society's precarious finances. Some very accomplished artists living in the county were not submitting work to the LAS because the exhibition quality was too variable from year to year, or so it was felt. It was resolved to contact the Boston and Sleaford Art Societies to propose a 'Lincolnshire Federation' of art groups so that the LAS could genuinely claim to represent the whole county. Meanwhile, lecturers from the Lincoln colleges were invited to submit works. We will see what became of these initiatives.

1972 Spring Fever Strikes Again

Nobody could accuse the LAS of inflexibility. Yet again the committee, under Wilson, decided on a change of title for the Spring Exhibition. This year it would be 'Drawings and Crafts'. Not content with her wall plaques the previous autumn, Mrs. Daisy Smith now introduced her lamp-bases, and Avril Morris contributed some stoneware 'Pagoda Forms'. The ceramics of Avril Morris are in the great tradition of English porcelain, and she was coming to the fore in the LAS. Joan Mostyn Lewis, a member since the 1930's, showed views of Grimsby and Barton on Humber while Ian Fraser contributed his 'Monte S. Angelo' series of drawings.

The Autumn Exhibition

The October 21st – November 19th Exhibition was again bereft of Bartl, but Mrs. Brough had visited the old lighthouse once owned by Peter Scott, near Sutton Bridge, and showed her watercolours of it. When he exhibited with the LAS in 1938, Scott was little known, but now he was one of the most televised people in Britain. There were many new names in the exhibition at both ends of the scale, the late E. W. Waldron showing three Wiltshire subjects, while Miss Jane Smith appeared for the Society's new Junior Section. A most intriguing pair of paintings came from W.R. Macdonald: 'Riot in Northern Ireland' and 'Explosion – Ulster '72'. These were amongst the first exhibits at the LAS to explore burning contemporary issues. Meanwhile, the usual names exhibited their tried and tested subjects – something that would become a problem as the decade closed, but for the time being, the Society's topographical watercolourists led a charmed life…

There were 167 exhibits this year. The number was creeping upwards yet again.

Boston and Sleaford Stay Silent

Williams' letters to the Boston and Sleaford Art Societies might as well have disappeared into a black hole, for no replies were forthcoming, and it was concluded that the sense of geographical identity and pride that existed then, and still exists now – may have generated suspicion about the Committee's initiatives. It may be remembered that those societies which had once affiliated to the LAS were in turn disaffiliated from it in 1956 by the LAS itself. Such events are not forgotten, and debates about quality were raging at that time. In this deafening silence the LAS braced itself for an explosion from Members having resolved to tighten the selection process as a sign to the County that only the very best was shown at the Usher. Meanwhile, one of the Society's Olympians was preparing for a show of his own – Tony Bartl.

1973 Bartl Rules OK

Coinciding with the Society's Spring Exhibition, the Usher presented an exhibition of Bartl's Drawings and Paintings, from March 30th – April 22nd. Marchbank Salmon, now one of the Society's historic monuments, returned from Croydon to open it, no doubt reminding his audience that he had brought Bartl to Lincoln. The most consistently admired of all LAS members – 'Head and Shoulders above the rest,' as some said, reminded Lincoln of his mastery of the brooding seascape in six Norfolk Coast subjects, and tossed in a few of his unrivalled portraits for good measure.

Meanwhile in a nearby room, the mortals did their bit for Drawings and Crafts, a name which had clearly come to stay for several years. Junior member Jane Smith contributed a study entitled 'Me and You'. Miss Massingberd-Mundy, a member of one of the County's oldest families, opened the exhibition on March 23rd.

The Autumn Exhibition

This was opened by Sir John Dudding on October 27th but no guest critic was identified in the minutes. The new Junior Members section was growing and Gill Nadin's contributions sounded and perhaps even smelled as good as they looked: 'Persian Roses', 'Strawberry Punnet', and 'Foam Bath'. 274 works were submitted.

The Need for Economies

The catalogue of the Autumn exhibition was produced at the Society's expense. On January 30th Wood had written to Williams to say that the Usher's Exhibition Fund was sadly overspent, and suggested that the Society might fund its own catalogues, with any income going into the Society's funds. The Usher would still provide publicity, and the usual 10% commission on sales would still go to the Society. But the cost of loan exhibitions was rising every year, and the grant given to the gallery was not enough to cover this, or the Exhibition Fund. As the decade progressed, the Society itself would have to make savings, duplicating forms and calendars of events rather than printing them, and considering a higher subscription.

Exhibition Rules Revised

The AGM on October 27th resolved the adoption of revised rules. Junior Membership would be limited to those between the age of 16-18 years, and the rules concerning selection of works for exhibitions were amended to enable a new category of 'doubtful' works as well as those clearly 'accepted' or 'rejected'. When all other voting had been completed, the 'doubtful' category works would be looked at and voted on again. Other new rules concerning the presentation and labelling of works were also introduced.

It was recorded that 20 Members and friends enjoyed a weekend in Norwich based at the University of East Anglia in September.

A Change of Name for the Second Time

In line with recent local government re-organisation, the LAS decided at the AGM to change its name to THE LINCOLNSHIRE AND SOUTH HUMBERSIDE ARTISTS' SOCIETY with effect from April 1st 1974. The new name lasted for almost 20 years and was removed on April 1st 1993, but the Regional Arts body, 'Lincolnshire and Humberside Arts', was a grant-awarding organisation which had been operating since the mid '60's, originally with Gribble on its Visual Arts Panel, and it gave grants to the Society but not to individuals unless they were holding sponsored exhibitions. The LHA dissolved in 1991, having helped the Society on many occasions.

1974 A Bumper Harvest

It had been resolved at the October '73 AGM that the new Exhibition rules would become effective from January 1st. Williams had primed the Members in his Reports, but neither he nor Wood could anticipate the largest submission – 319 works – the Annual Exhibition had seen for many years. Of these, only 199 were accepted by the now 'scrupulously careful' committee, which meant many disappointed or outraged artists, and their ranks were swelled in '74 by 16 new Full Members elevated from the Associate level, including Robin Wheeldon, whose engaging style echoed Victorian academic painting especially when he painted animals. His father John had a well-known art shop, gallery and framing business on the Strait in Lincoln and was an accomplished artist in his own right, though he never joined the Society. In Monica Smith's time however, he did have a number of his own works hung in the LAS exhibitions when poor overall submissions meant that gaps needed to be filled. Miss Smith would dash across from the Usher to see what John had got! One new Associate in '74 was A. J. Ludlam who had won many painting prizes after graduating from Grimsby, Camberwell and the Royal Academy Schools. He was quickly made a Full Member in '75.

Charles Speed, *Cottingham Church*

The Spring Exhibition

Again, 'Of Drawing and Crafts' featured 4 drawings by new Full Member P. T. Bendelow, and 4 screenprints and photographic prints by Paton, which again called the title of the Exhibition into question. Bartl made two contributions and Oyler 4, including a drawing of Harlech Castle. In her many decades with the LAS, she covered the entire British Isles. Tom Baker, the LAS Vice-President, opened the Exhibition and the Annual Report states that it was well attended and that 14 works were sold, although the 'uncertainty about the precise aim or character of this particular exhibition' still 'needed to be resolved'.

The Autumn Exhibition - October 19th – November 17th

After the most difficult selection process for many years, 199 works were hung from 319 entries. Two Bartl portraits attracted a lot of attention, one being of John Piper (who had visited Lincoln that year and had enjoyed a meeting with the Wheeldons at Waddington) and the other of Lincoln's Dean, Oliver Fiennes. Paton showed 4 landscapes and Joan Lock, a new Associate, showed for the first time. She was a graduate of Sheffield School

of Art, and went on to the Royal College which in her time was evacuated to the Lake District. A fine print maker, she was a lively exponent of the elimination method of lino-cutting, and was influenced by Vuillard, Vermeer, Gauguin and Matisse. Ian Fraser was given a solo exhibition between the Society's two shows and presented his architectural paintings, including Assisi, between June and July.

1975 Fresh Faces and Rejected Faces

From March 1st, David Morris succeeded Williams as Secretary, while Williams continued as Treasurer. A lecturer in Ceramics at Grimsby, Morris had been brought into the Society by his colleague Paton. He and his wife Avril ensured that LAS exhibitions would contain a diversity of ceramics alongside Blatherwick's stoneware, and as Secretary he had to deal with a number of indignant reactions from artists whose works were rejected from the exhibitions, bringing tact and reassurance to his responses.

Judith Oyler became Social Secretary at this time, a role which she had, in effect, played for several years, and her letters are full of catering suggestions and a warm concern for the wellbeing of members.

'Miss Dudding's Outcry'

Richard Wood wrote to Morris in December enclosing a breakdown of acceptances and rejections for the Autumn Exhibition. 'This followed Miss Dudding's outcry over her work being rejected,' added Wood. In fact, 6 Full Members had experienced total rejection in 1975, so Dudding was not alone, but she had suffered total rejection before, and this must have seemed harsh.

Fury and Indignation

Then came the Morton affair. Rose Morton, a recent Associate, was a highly qualified and successful artist, as were so many who at this period were required initially to join as Associates. Her one submission to the Autumn

Exhibition had been rejected, so her husband and some of their supporters withdrew their works in protest and wrote scathing letters to the committee questioning its competence. Morris replied, explaining that this was regrettable since the committee, fully aware of Rose's talent, had invited her to submit more work for consideration for Full Membership, but even as he read out in committee a protest letter from a Morton supporter, Mr. Lester George, George had entered the Usher and removed his work.

Williams recalls indignation and fury and a number of resignations over the issue of rejected works. He was 'phoned at home by Members demanding to know why their work had been rejected, and Geoffrey Wilson, who was actually neutral in his position, was also 'assailed by a number of irate members, not only on the 'phone but face to face!'

Although no minutes can be found to prove the visit in 1974 of Peter Todd, Head of Fine Art at Grimsby, Williams recalls that Todd (a dedicated naturalistic painter) 'fiercely attacked any abstract work in the show', with 'remarks so scathing that it was feared younger members would withdraw'. Fortunately, none did. Dudding's work was highly praised by Todd, but ironically, as Morris and Paton remember, she had rushed out of the Criticism, fearing the worst, as Todd came ever nearer to her work!

The Spring Exhibition of Drawings and Crafts (March 22nd – April 20th) had 139 exhibits and 9 sales and was opened by D. Witney, the Headmaster of Edward VI Grammar School in Louth.

The Autumn Exhibition (October 18th – November 16th) had 193 exhibits and featured several oddly titled works by Lester George (before he removed them) along with 3 Ludlams, Oyler wafting in from Provence with 'Wild Lavender', and one Bartl, 'The Sand and the Sea', while new Associate, Richard Devereux, who would become

Peter Williams, *Passage From The Nelson Mass: "Et Incarnatus"*

one of Lincolnshire's most admired artists, contributed 'Funny Looks'. Clifford Ellis, the notable book illustrator, had been invited to criticise the 1975 Exhibition, but at the last minute he was unable to come, and David Ainley of Matlock stepped into the breach. Ellis came in 1976.

There were now 75 Full Members and thrice that number of Associates, so with many Young Members beginning to make notable contributions, the hopes of Williams and Wood at the beginning of the '70's seemed close to being realised. However, early in 1975, Williams reported a fall in the membership and referred to 'financial ills' which would need to be tackled by 'cutting one's cloth'.

1976 Ladderback Chairs and an Arthritic Carob Tree

Richard Woods' fears that the Usher would have to close on Mondays were realised on April 1st. The Monday closure would remain in force for 28 years. Meanwhile Gill Nadin (or Gill Foot as she was frequently called

Gill Nadin, *Pears With Dark Plums*

Gill Nadin, *River Slea*

following her marriage) had become Chairman, while Lord Ancaster gave notice of his intention to retire as President, his handwriting in the unmistakable vivid green ink becoming ever shakier, to be succeeded by the Hon. Edward Cust in 1977. Rose Morton recovered from the problems of 1975, and exhibited following her elevation to Full Membership, along with Joan Lock and David Tarttelin. The Spring Exhibition was preceded by a

revealing committee meeting at which Nadin agreed to provide a work for a raffle suggested by Wilson, who had experienced success with raffles in previous years. 'Miss Oyler registered her disapproval of this kind of activity,' while Morris said it was boring, but that if it went ahead, 'a licence should be applied for in order to widen the scope'. Obviously, Oyler was not prepared to go all the way down her social secretary's road!

The Exhibition of Drawings and Crafts

The Exhibition held from March 20th – April 18th found Dudding showing 19th century Cathedral Plate Designs. She was a regular worshipper at the Cathedral and helped out there whenever she could. Anyone interested in trees would have enjoyed this show, for H. F. Gosney, a sculptor who enjoyed portraying his garden, showed three tree drawings, while J. Nottage showed 'Silver Birches' and Pamela Hughes presented her 'Arthritic Carob Tree'. Dorothy Turner showed two ladderback chairs she had made, and Sheila Wyatt showed two cement-fondue figures. Rounding out this varied show, Dudding displayed her prowess in etching with 'The Camber, Portsmouth'. But she seems to have avoided the Autumn Exhibition, in case her work was rejected yet again. Open from October 16th to November 14th, this had 168 exhibits including four 'Dancing Ladies' by Avril Morris, four portrait paintings by Robin Wheeldon, four 'Fragments of a House' by Nadin, and four Sheila Parkinsons of Boston Stump and the Lincolnshire landscape. The tendency to regard the four allowable submissions as an opportunity to do a series of works on a certain theme may also have established itself as a way of getting all four works accepted.

1976 also saw a substantial travelling exhibition to Scunthorpe and Gainsborough with 119 exhibits. Nadia Eadie charged £100 each for her oils of 'The Rockery' and 'Poinsettia' but a mere £12 would have purchased Dudding's drawing of three Cathedral Choristers.

Morris Warns About Quality

During the Spring Exhibition, a bowl by Mrs. P. E. Simpson, rejected by the committee, mysteriously found its way into the show. Morris, himself an accomplished potter, felt that this precedent should not be tolerated, and wanted his protest recorded. He then commented on the low entry and falling standards in the submitted craftwork and called for a full discussion and review of the selection procedures.

1977 The Year of the Pencil

Outdoor sketching days were repeatedly proposed and organised by Judith Oyler at this period but minutes record that very few members took advantage, and a day in Horncastle attracted 20, but a day based at Diocesan House in Lincoln in June '77 struggled to meet required numbers. Despite this it seems many drawings were available for the Spring Exhibition which this year was from March 19th to April 17th. Echo critic Wilham Varcoe declared that 'many pencil studies make this exhibition rewarding' and he particularly admired Robin Wheeldon's four 'Contrasting Faces', and Nadin's four drawings of children, which he felt to be outstanding. Iona Cartwright showed two Arab Mares, while Alma Paget showed four Northumberland Views, and Zakrzewski had obviously been to Rome, drawing its churches, with Dudding (still either avoiding or being rejected from, the Autumn shows) contributing a drawing of St. Martin's Square in Lincoln. Varcoe felt that the pots of Blatherwick and the Morrises were 'examples of conscientious craftsmanship'.

The Autumn Exhibition

190 exhibits greeted the public between October 15th and November 13th. Jill Marschner contributed three intriguing works: 'Peat Dig', 'Grey Moor' and 'Brown Moor'. Wilson had been to Normandy and Gorleston, and Nina Banham contributed a mosaic fish. Ian Simpson, Principal of St. Martin's Art College of Art, London, opened the exhibition and gave a Criticism of some of the paintings exhibited.

At the AGM on October 15th the Earl of Ancaster retired as President with the heartfelt thanks of 44 members and a specially commissioned drawing by Peter Brannan, presented to The Earl by Chairman Gill Nadin. He had been President for many years from 1961 – 1977 and had inspired great affection.

Robin Wheeldon, *Combine Harvesting at Boothby Pagnall, 1999*

Group Exhibitions for Prominent Members

The Usher held two exhibitions in '77 featuring LAS stalwarts and running concurrently. Wilson and Paton, with their shared passion for coastal landscapes, exhibited from February 4th – March 6th, while Tarttelin, Gosney and C. Pratt exhibited from February 5th.

1978 Mysterious Nudes

Mrs. Audsley Power, a distinguished portraitist from Sleaford described by Paton as 'that magnificent woman' succeeded Gill Nadin as Chairman. Overtures were made again to the architects of Lincolnshire, after several had expressed a desire to exhibit with the LAS, and at first no reply was forthcoming from the Lincolnshire Society of Architects, so the overture had to be performed again in 1979. Meanwhile, 1978 was the Hon. Edward Cust's only year as President, illness having prevented his participation. Elected to Full Membership were J.B. Anderson, Ann Atkinson, Bernard Brewer (who had taken over as Secretary from Morris in October 1976), Dr. W. P. Haigh, Rosie Hawes, Pamela Hughes, the Rev. H. B. Pruen, and Sidney Wright. In 1979 Brewer was to receive a very distressing 'phone call from Wright making some very disappointing remarks about certain committee members and the way the affairs of the Society were handled. As a result, Wright was not elected onto the committee! Wright may have had some valid points, for during the next five years critical assessments of the LAS in the press would indicate that sound judgement was perhaps being relaxed despite the continuing success of the exhibitions. Bartl's sensuous and mysterious nudes appearing in the Spring and Autumn shows, seemed the only exhibits to excite a considered response from another Echo critic Stephen Paterson.

Mud in Your Eye

The Spring Exhibition (April 8th – May 7th) contained 138 exhibits, the only intriguing title being Hollinshead's charcoal of 'Hawk against a Window'. The Autumn Exhibition (October 7th) had 148 paintings and seven pots, described by Paterson as 'A bit of a hotchpotch', but 'Art for all tastes'. Various snow scenes included P. Brannan's 'Snowscene' and Valentine's 'A Copse across Snowfield', while V. R. Williamson offered 'Lancaster over Wartime Skellingthorpe'. Readers of the Echo were invited to choose between a painting costing over £100, and a biscuit barrel costing only £4.50, by David Morris, and Nina Banham's 'Mud, Mud, Mud' was an eye-catcher. But Paterson sounded a familiar alarm: 'The Abstract section seems badly under-represented'. Somehow, the achievement of the '60's had slipped.

In May 1978 Judith Oyler was to have been given a solo exhibition at the Usher, but she felt that she could not exhibit alone, so Audsley Power and the Morrises were invited to join her. In the autumn of her life, Oyler still resisted the spotlight, preferring to feel that others were fairly treated and that her friend Mary Dudding in particular was allowed to have at least one work in the travelling exhibitions, even if this meant withdrawing her own.

1979 Williams says Farewell

The LAS had already assisted the Lincolnshire Old Churches Trust with an art exhibition at the 1976 Lincolnshire Show, and it continued to display paintings at the Show, joining the Museums complex in '79 at the invitation of Mr. R. A. Gunstone. Power, Pruen, Bartl, Williams and Nadin organised the transportation of some 92 exhibits which were displayed over three days in late June. The Society had covenanted £10 a year for seven years to the Lincoln Cathedral Fabric Fund, and received a letter of appreciation from Sir Francis Hill and the Dean and Chapter, but Williams noted that far too much was being spent on wine at the exhibitions. Members were urged to submit more work to the exhibitions and encourage friends to join, for despite the 74 Full Members recorded in May 1979 it was felt that around 19 would not renew their subscriptions. Williams retired as Treasurer on November 10th, having accepted the Principal's job at Medway, and Bernard Brewer decided to take the Treasurer's job temporarily.

The Spring Exhibition (March 17th – April 16th) was rejuvenated with a new large format catalogue. 110 exhibits included four Patons of which two were watercolours of Nocton Fen, while Dudding showed 'Winter Aconites' and 'Lilies'. Oyler had gone to the edge and returned with 'Cliff Edge, Isle of Man' and 'Cliff Edge, Handa Island'.

The Autumn Exhibition (October 13th – November 11th) was opened by Carel Weight CBA, RA, who was faced with 178 exhibits including a 'token Dudding', of Lincoln's Old Palace Gateway, and Ann Atkinson's 'Les Preludes from a theme of Liszt', while young G. M. Bauer, now a Full Member, showed 'Cat on a Wall'.

7

The 1980's - Tradition and Innovation

Gill Ross-Kelsey, *Garden Pond I*

Richard Devereux, *Untitled, 1995*

The 1980's saw an increasing polarisation of traditional, mostly landscape, work and innovative explorations of subject and approach. While women members employed a dazzling variety of media including handmade paper, embroidery, slate and plastics, many of the men shifted their geographical locations rather than their painterly language. A handful transcended the familiar traditional approach, and Marschner, the new Chairman, devised new ways to engage the public at large with the products of the LAS. A pronounced social dimension flourished, with enterprising suppers combined with Openings which were provided by a dedicated team of members, and there were more evenings of art films, devised by Dick Coon. And this was also the decade of Noel Black, the Society's most significant sculptor since Grimble, who joined in 1983 and became Chairman as the decade closed. Tom Baker became President in 1983 after Lord Brownlow's few years in that office, and a new and supremely effective Treasurer was elected in the person of Charles Speed, who had already exhibited with the LAS.

A Study in Contrasts

Charles Speed became Treasurer in April 1980. An accountant at Ruston's, he was persuaded by his friend Bernard Brewer, who was still Secretary, to undertake a role which had not hitherto, in his view, been very well done. Apparently, so-called Balance Sheets had been merely summaries of receipts and payments and did not, in Speed's view, convey a complete picture of the Society's affairs. At the AGM, Speed expressed his disapproval and promised better things. Speed, the ideal exponent of the pleasing watercolour, and representing perhaps many of the traditional members, could not get on with Bartl, who hardly ever acknowledged him. It must have been equally difficult for Bartl, who really wanted to get rid of the traditional work of the Sunday painters and made no secret of it. He was surrounded at every show by admirers, and eventually Speed ventured to enquire of the Committee why Bartl's work always occupied the centre of the main wall in Gallery One. This

Geoff Smith, *Four Horses On Hillside (Mixed Media)*

was met by 'a wall of silence'. Speed's attitude towards Bartl represented the artistic battles the Society had fought for so long and which obviously caused problems at exhibitions. One remark by Speed is especially telling: 'I learned of Bartl's unseen dominance of the Society'. Yet this dominance seems in the main to have been to the benefit of the LAS, for artists as diverse as Nadin and Hollinshead had expressed their debt to Bartl, as had all his students.

The Speed-Bartl situation exemplified the two major polarities in the Society and gave it a healthy creative tension. The LAS has not, thus far, experienced a split resulting in another society devoted purely to Abstraction, as happened in St. Ives when Barbara Hepworth, Ben Nicholson and others left the St. Ives Society to form the Penwith Society. Lincolnshire's reluctance to divide seems to stem from a 'Society feeling' that was expressed by Nadin in 1993: 'We like to

Dr. Joseph Smedley, *Cat's Eden*

The Autumn Exhibition opened October 13th and was criticised by Bernard Dunstan RA, who was very impressed but said his 'only criticism was the almost total lack of abstract painting' – a familiar refrain! Stephen Paterson, in the Echo, wrote of 'landscapes that were much of a muchness…and paintings of tigers'. The prints were praised, as was the consistency in the use of colour: 'Nothing raucous or violent'. Bartl's and Wilson's sea paintings were praised in the Chronicle as 'poetic statements', while Alan Bruce's paintings showed 'flowers more adventurously explored than usual', and John Mitchinson's four 'fine oils' were 'studies in depth, of spatial relationship'. The show's popularity was borne out by 46 sales, 16 more than 1979. The exhibitions at the Lincolnshire Show, now in their fourth year, and at the Richmond Park Gallery in Gainsborough meant that paintings were out of the artists' hands for three or four months, and Mrs. Brough wondered whether this could be avoided, but Marschner pointed out that the scheduling of the shows made it impracticable for works to be returned and re-submitted.

Calls for a new Life Class

At the October AGM Mr. Pridgeon called for the reintroduction of life classes and expressed his willingness to organise them. 12 members supported this. When Williams had left, his successor had been Derek Hawker, of whom there is no mention in the minutes. Clearly the Art College link had broken after Williams had worked successfully to restore it. But Williams had always stood up to the authorities and had steered his own ship, as Gribble had done before him, whereas Hawker was thought by many to be easier for the County Council to deal with. Marschner told Pridgeon that a hall off Lincoln's Newport could be available for the life classes, which had formerly always been at the Art College. The matter was investigated, and a series of life-classes was indeed held.

The other interesting event for the LAS in 1980 was an exhibition for the Lincolnshire Art Supporters Club, at

be a melting-pot with the traditional and the avant-garde'.

The 1980 Spring Exhibition was given a new name for the new decade: Paintings in Watercolours, Drawings and Crafts. With 138 exhibits it ran from March 15th to April 13th and was opened by Maurice Sheppard, the vice president of the Royal Watercolour Society, who had been recommended by Carel Weight.

Knaith Hall, near Gainsborough, from May 15th. All the exhibitors were LAS members and Wilson remembers that there were ten double screens of work, and numerous sales, with a good attendance.

1981 75th Anniverary

It had been hoped to hold an Anniversary Dinner at Lord Brownlow's Belton House, but on October 23rd Lord and Lady Brownlow found themselves at the Usher for a smaller affair than had been hoped, and only a fortnight before, Marschner had expressed the committee's disappointment that only 28 tickets had so far been sold. When asked to indicate how many more would come if the dress code was relaxed, nobody responded. But Tom Baker brushed up on the Society's history for his speech, Wilson typically enjoyed the evening as Chairman yet again, and Brownlow presided. Those who came greatly enjoyed the opportunity to socialise.

The 1981 Spring Exhibition had 145 exhibits and 25 sales, and Members were warned not to submit works in acrylics or oils. Despite what Brewer described as 'a year of recession', sales had been buoyant, but the Autumn Exhibition generated 26 sales, 20 fewer than 1980. this occasion was graced by the presence of Opener-Critic, Roger de Grey RA, who saw 200 works by 70 artists. Bartl, Wilson and Speed had depicted the English coast at Holkham, Walberswick and Cornwall respectively, while Alison Wilson and Alan Bruce continued in a floral vein, Bruce's 'Fen House Daisies' being a stunning essay in light and shadow. Hollinshead showed a mysterious drawing of two trout while the local surrealist Dr. Aldridge Haddock made a contribution. Gill Kelsey's 'Sand Dune Grasses' were a quartet of sensitive swirling studies, while G. E. Smith's Matisse-like 'Flower Pickers '81' was full of life and light. Doris Hartley contributed a fine Bloomsbury-style 'Portrait of Louie'. But Bartl's darkly dramatic 'Portrait of Caroline' was more riveting. Fenella Stoner, a new Associate Member with a nursing background who had belonged to various art societies in London, weighed in with domestic studies combining

Dick Coon, *Untitled*

psychological elements with a virile compositional flair, as in 'Catnap'. Robin Wheeldon showed ploughing scenes, and perhaps the darkest title came from D. J. Dunthorne: 'Oh woman'.

Honorary Members

On October 10th, Vice President, Tom Baker and 50 members elected Judith Oyler and Clive Browne Honorary Members 'in recognition of their long and valued service to the Society'. Browne's oils and Oyler's watercolours of the Lincolnshire landscape had been admired in the LAS

Sue Hayward, *Hand-made Paper*

exhibitions and in London, for several decades.

1982 'A Big Rift'

On June 19th, Lucy Marschner, E. L. Littlewood, Francis le Marchant, John Grey, Helen Webber and Dick Coon were made Full Members. Dick Coon was on the staff of the Art College. A superb draughtsman and a stimulating teacher, he was to organise several successful video evenings for the LAS. He felt there were parallels to music in his abstracts, whose colour was *'like bunches*

of notes affecting the emotions'. But in 1982, le Marchant would dazzle at the Autumn Exhibition with a painting so large it required 'special dispensation' as Wilson recalled, to be exhibited.

Even Varcoe was inspired to abandon his usual balanced tones, pronouncing le Marchant's panorama of Todi 'formidable,' though he also found Bartl's large portrait of Peter Hodgkinson 'strong and determined' and hailed Blatherwick's work as 'pottery of the utmost refinement'.

Varcoe went on to say that Peter Brannan's 'stark impression of 'Snow at Welbourne' is the best of many local scenes in the show', but that Barrell's delicate watercolours of Chichester Harbour and Bosham were good, and the figurative paintings of new Associate, Nick Ellerby had 'vibrancy'. William Bowyer RA opened and commented on the exhibition on November 12th but there is no record of his opinions. Max Marschner showed strong figure studies, but mining the traditional vein deeply came Robin Wheeldon's 'Spaniel and Hare' and Speed's 'Boats at Blakeney'. Woad's 'Scarborough Harbour' offered exciting abstract patterns. Varcoe's overall judgement still resonates: 'there is a big rift between the excellent and the less impressive' – words which were not lost on Richard Wood, who had been worrying about the overall appearance of the LAS exhibitions for some time. Formerly, works had been hung several deep, but Wood temporarily insisted on a tidier, clearer hanging of all works on one line, resulting in only 129 pictures being chosen for 1982.

Busy Years

With four major exhibitions each year, the Society was operating at maximum stretch, and so were its caterers in the persons of Gill Nadin, Jill Marschner, Angela Brewer, Thirza Wilson and Fenella Stoner. Other pitched in with their support and suppers of beef and beer were a tempting traditional Lincolnshire inducement to attend Openings. Grimble and Whitaker had the lion's share of work over the Lincolnshire Show Exhibition which had 79 exhibits in '82, while the Richmond Park Exhibition at Gainsborough had 55 exhibits. The Society's thoughts turned to the future and to an assessment of its indebtedness to the Usher Gallery, which was experiencing ever more calls on its spaces and time-slots.

1983 Changing Strategies

Geoffrey Wilson, now well into his second term as Chairman, told his committee on March 19th that the LAS had enjoyed two exhibitions a year at the Usher since 1962.

It was agreed that in 1985 the Society should revert back to the original idea of one major Usher exhibition per year, and that the Annual Exhibitions should run for six weeks towards the latter part of the year. The gallery would still be available for meetings and selection sessions for all the Society's exhibitions, and would still assist with the supply of screens, plinths and so forth wherever possible.

The Studio Fund finds resolution at last

Charles Speed relished his job as Treasurer and worked with Brewer and his successor in '84, Dr. Joe Smedley, to change the Constitution, creating the offices of Membership Secretary, with Rosie Bradshaw as the first to be appointed, and Exhibitions Secretary with Gill Nadin. Many Members were not paying their subscriptions, and Speed undertook a thorough and very pointed purge, feeling rightly that 'being very valuable members' did not entitle people to forget paying. He was also concerned that the £1,290 deposited in the bank as the Studio Fund should be preserved, and issued a detailed statement suggesting a resolution that the Fund should now be called the Capital Reserve Fund, since the sum on deposit would never allow the purchase of any studio premises.

The Spring Exhibition coincided exactly with a new venture, a Lincoln Festival Exhibition, which Marschner organised with a pantechnicon to be parked in the Cathedral Eastgate area and used as a walk-in art gallery. Both exhibitions began on April 30th, and the Festival show reflected Marschner's conviction that art should be a part of the community. Adapted wire coat-hangers were used to secure the paintings to the walls of the pantechnicon.

The 1983 Autumn Exhibition was opened and criticised by Ken Howard ARA, RWS, who by common consent is regarded as the best guest critic the Society has had in living memory. Howard spoke to as many members as possible, and his helpful comments left a lasting impression. He was invited back again, in 1998. But in the Echo, Varcoe's knives were out. 'A somewhat overstocked show containing many well-worn ideas' was his judgement on this 'generally predictable' exhibition. He felt that David Kitching's 'Daniel' 'an excellent study of leather-jacketted youth casting a quizzical eye at society' was 'easily the most thought provoking and arresting piece'. Roper's atmospheric watercolour of 'Branston Fen', M. A. Toomer's 'Nocton' and J. B. Horner's work were the only other items given Varcoe's approval. Bartl did not exhibit, but Noel Black, the new Associate sculptor, showed 'Homage to Tennyson', I and II. As usual, a vast tide of coastal subjects was shown by most of the other members, but one particularly fine exponent alongside Bartl was Ken Lamming, the art master at the Girl's Grammar School in Brigg. He produced experimental reliefs, pierced and layered, to do with beaches and wave formations.

Usher Practicalities

Richard Wood recalled that every effort was made to avoid the 'somewhat overstocked' show. He was often given the final say about any 'doubtful' submissions if the voting was equal, but he would also remove work by Full Members which the hanging committee had already accepted, which meant that it had to be voted on again. The physical work generated by the LAS exhibitions was considerable, with up to 400 submissions all of which had to be temporarily stored. Wood favoured, and introduced, the idea of work hung on one line rather than several deep, but pressures on space especially if only two rooms were available, meant that groups of related works had to be hung one above the other. The LAS always recognised the work of the Usher staff and warm appreciation was always recorded in committee and at every AGM.

Chill October

As the year died, it took two of the Society's greatest members with it – Francis Cooper and Judith Oyler. Grace Cooper wrote to Brewer from Lowestoft on

Noel Black, *Steel Form*

September 11th to say what a great comfort his letter of condolence, on the Society's behalf, had been. She added, poignantly, *'Frank thought the world of Peter and his paintings, always forecasting a great future.'* This was a reference to Peter Brannan and we have already seen the accuracy of Cooper's forecast. Gill Nadin announced the passing of Judith Oyler, whose funeral took place in Lincoln Cathedral on October 2nd, and referred to the

Nick Ellerby, *Alice*

beautiful floral tributes including one from the Society. She had exhibited with and served her Society for over 40 years and had come to almost every event despite pain. 'We miss her forthright sense of humour,' added Nadin, and it was proposed that the interest from the Studio Fund be used to fund the Judith Oyler Memorial Prize for the most meritorious work on show in an LAS exhibition. This was first won by Keith Roper in 1985. Miss Oyler's last exhibit was 'Low Tide, Anglesey'. That tide had taken her.

...And a Hopeful Dawn...

Gill Nadin, forever upbeat, issued the most buoyant of messages in the New Year:

'Greetings for 1984! May the year be fruitful for you – remembering that as your immediate past Chairman, Geoffrey Wilson, always says 'The Art is the Thing.'

The Spring Exhibition (March 17th – April 15th) was the last to be held at the Usher before it appeared in other county venues. There were 153 exhibits. Marschner was looking into a fresh idea for the Lincoln Festival whereby paintings could be exhibited on the railings in Castle Square, using batons and clear sheeting, but this did not take place. Sadly, Smedley reported that the response had been somewhat disappointing. He had taken over as Secretary from Bernard Brewer, whose clashes with Nadin in committee had taken their toll. For the next seven years Smedley would be a very conscientious Secretary.

1984 Criticism from Within

Richard Wood had felt for some time that there had indeed been an uneven quality in the LAS exhibitions and that this was detrimental to the Usher's standing. Morris and Paton recalled that an Art Society in Sussex had actually lost its venue because of the inclusion of inferior work in its exhibitions. The 1984 Exhibition provoked a strong letter from Wood to Nadin. Writing in the Echo, Chris Sharpe, an 'old boy of the College of Art' (1952-56) contributed a criticism which contained the main reason for Wood's concern. Although he said the show was 'splendidly up to scratch', he felt that Lucy Marschner, Dick Coon and Alan Price 'stand out from the sea of watercolours and occasional sculptures'. Sharpe was enthusiastic about Nadin's 'gifted and exciting' work, Hollinshead's 'mystic and stylish' images and Wilson's 'charming seascapes', but felt, as Varcoe had done the previous year, that Kitching again stole the show with another 'outrageous punk rocker'. The opinion of Opener Stanislas Frenkiel, Reader Emeritus of the University of London, is not recorded but he did call for a Lincoln Arts Centre, echoing Dick Taverne's plea of years earlier, and with the same result.

Asif Kamal, *Fossil Seekers*

Steve Wallhead, *Stoneware Covered Jar*

Wood's Letter

After the Autumn Show, Wood's letter was read out to members. He objected strongly to the Society exhibiting or being forced by the membership to exhibit inferior work merely to avoid hurting the feelings of a few of its members. As an 'area Society', he went on, its exhibitions should draw the cream of the various artists and groups together. He wondered, also, whether there should be a stricter method of joining the Society rather than merely paying a subscription. His words were weighed and eventually acted upon.

Instructive and Inspiring Evenings

Dick Coon walked around the Autumn Exhibition with Nick Ellerby, and remarked that looking at the works on show, you would never think that half of the art movements of the 20th century had ever taken place. In an attempt to remedy this, his video evenings, which Speed found expensive, were designed to stimulate interest in art debates, techniques and significant modernists. Alison Wilson remembers that they were so inspirational that after the film on various printing techniques, she got busy in her studio utilising the advice. Members learned about Kurt Schwitters' time in the Lake District, minority art and mass culture, and Carel Weight, a recent Opener Critic.

Finally for 1984, while the committee and Membership were digesting Wood's ultimatum, honorary membership was bestowed on Tony Bartl, and Wilson settled into his new home in Norfolk, having resigned from the Committee because of the travelling problems his move entailed.

1985 A Slap in the Face

Never one to mince words, Speed issued a memo to all members of the committee on June 6th. It is the most stinging document in the LAS's history but perhaps it had to be written. Speed literally lost his temper on paper, deriding the buying of catalogues at 53 pence each only to sell them at 20 pence. He tore into several Members by name for repeated non-payment of subscriptions and informed the committee that he was deleting the names of 33 Associates as a result. He reached his climax in the middle of all this:

'On 31st December 1980 the Society was worth £430. By the 31st December 1984 we had succeeded in reducing that to £72, and all that after increasing the rate of subscriptions and the commission on sales'.

He demonstrated that the sudden resignation of his friend Brewer in 1984 had cost the Society more money, an oblique swipe, perhaps, at Nadin, whose indomitable force in committee had tried Brewer beyond endurance. These things happen, and Speed gave the Society a lot

101

Mary Fitzpayne, *The Wooden Horse*

to aim for, as did Nadin on the purely artistic front. Looking at the catalogues of the 1980's, nobody today would begrudge their cost, but Speed had the health of the LAS at heart.

Spring in Grimsby

Max Marschner, ever willing to further the Society's interest whether helping with catering, catalogue design, photography or committee work, now drove a hired vehicle to Grimsby, stuffed with exhibits for the Spring Exhibition. The show opened in Grimsby's Central Library on March 9th and was so successful that several visitors decided to join the Society. But there were few sales and the cost of mounting the exhibition was a problem, so a hanging fee, chargeable in the event of work being accepted, was proposed and accepted for future shows.

1985 Autumn Exhibition – On Safari in Lincoln Cathedral

Opened by William Varley, Art Critic of the Guardian, on November 17th, the exhibition had 196 exhibits, and made 31 sales. Everyone was pleased with the standard, and the Marschner family were out in force, with Jill in the Appenines, Lucy portraying 'Sheep grazing' and 'Beast', and Max presenting four linocuts of various animals carved in the stonework of the Cathedral, presented under the title 'On Safari in Lincoln Cathedral'. It was a different and refreshing way of looking at the Society's principal motif. There were lots of girls pictured in this show, too – Ellerby presenting several of his psychologically charged portraits enabling the viewer to enter their world, Nadin showing 'Girl at Window', and Ison examining several more girls. Four Noel Brannans explored tangled or broken objects, while Gill Ross presented a monotype of 'Water Gardens' and Coon explored 'Light and Water at Stoupe Beck'. Morris had a rest from his ceramics and presented 4 farm studies, and it was left to Nadia Eadie to bat for the abstractionists with four abstract figures, in chalk.

The AGM on November 16th had Miss Dudding complaining about the loss of the Spring Exhibitions from the Usher, maintaining that tourists were thereby deprived of the chance of seeing works of Lincolnshire Artists, and there was a possible loss of income from sales that could have been made. Smedley gave the first inkling that the committee were thinking about the problems of the two tier membership system and perhaps replacing it with a single form of membership, but at subsequent meetings members expressed their satisfaction with the two tier structure because it gave them something to aim for, and stimulated better standards. The debate would rage for another eight years. Mary Dudding was congratulated on her solo show in the Usher in November.

1986 A Shock in Stamford

The Spring Exhibition, continuing its nomadic existence at the Stamford Art Centre, realised 15 sales, but Keith Roper had noticed exhibits being removed from the walls during an antique fair. Moreover, the Arts Centre charged 20% commission, which extended to the sales of catalogues, losing the LAS £38. It omitted to tell the Society about this beforehand. As a result the LAS could not afford to mount its Summer Exhibition in Gainsborough, so everything depended on the Autumn Show at the Usher. Speed was pleased to report that although losses had been sustained over the buffet and the printing costs of the catalogue, the balance of accounts over the year had resulted in a favourable sum of £650.

Happy Zebras and Phallic Symbols

William Varcoe was also favourably disposed to the Society this year, and proclaimed 'a good overall standard'. Alan Humberston, Visual Arts Officer of Lincolnshire and Humberside Arts, was the Opener of the Autumn show on November 17th which featured 'other themes explored by more enterprising artists. A. P. Cahusac's 'Zebra Crossing', for instance, is not a street scene but a quartet of happy zebras. Varcoe also approved of Stoner's 'Study in White', Pruen's 'Study in Olive Green', and Joan Grimble's mosaics, and found Richard Ison's work strong in character and technique. And he bewailed the paucity of stoneware, unusual for the LAS, but found Jo Sloan's 'Phallic Symbol' and works by Noel Black a demonstration of 'their skill in ceramics'. The 'Phallic Symbol' was not for sale, but Dudding's 'A Lincoln Schoolboy' was – at a very high price for her, of £50. The 149 exhibits indicated that a rigorous selection process had occurred.

1987 A Society in Miniature

Max Marschner was 'at full throttle' in the early part of the year, organising and advertising the Spring Exhibition for the Lincoln Festival for which Members were invited to submit one small work on card or paper in a plastic casing, no larger than 4" by $5\frac{1}{2}$". In effect, these would present the LAS in miniature, with the idea that such a portable show could be hung in several different venues. It proved a great success. The Spring Exhibition had covered costs thanks to the hanging fee charged to members, but there had been no income from sales.

During the year, Smedley and Coon gave talks on the figure and colour respectively, which were much appreciated despite poor attendances. Smedley finally resigned as Secretary after four years and Janet Minty took over temporarily. Smedley's letters to members exhorting their increased involvement were warmly couched and give the impression he enjoyed his job. The committee gave him a generous book token in recognition of his contribution.

The Autumn Exhibition of 1987 was strong in sculpture and ceramics, with Black showing three 'Fissure' sculptures in steel and mahogany, and new member Steve Wallhead showing two stoneware items. Wallhead was a highly regarded potter who had been so impressed by the recent LAS exhibition in Stamford that he had decided to join the Society. Blatherwick showed three earthenware items and Susan Morrison showed two 'Heads' in mild steel and cast iron. The guest critic, Anthony Eyton RA of Camberwell, who had been invited and looked after by Gillian Ross Kelsey following her completion of her fine art degree there in the early 1970's, awarded the second Judith Oyler Prize to Peter Hammond for his gouache: 'Epiphany'. There were 190 exhibits with Max Marschner making a strong impression with two screenprints of luminous intensity: 'Lines of Poplars' and 'Trunks and Branches'. Varcoe also felt that Bartl and the Brannans contributed outstanding work and noticed Sue Hayward's work with handmade paper, string and threads. Her work had been accepted by the Royal Academy and she was becoming a popular and hardworking Full Member. 'The choice of media is wide,' said Varcoe, 'but the standard is variable'. Eyton agreed, and delivered a very robust criticism according to those present. Coon's message in the catalogue was unusual and worth quoting.

A Timely Message from the Chairman

Coon began sensitively with a thought that can only be roundly echoed today, when he said that

'Artists and Societies do not always go together…which makes the exhibition a considerable achievement in itself…any knowledgeable observer will notice that most of the major 20th century art movements are conspicuously under-represented or completely absent, and this suggests that the most necessary progress is towards a wider representation of the art most characteristic of our times and a welcoming of the exciting arguments which they inevitably stimulate.'

Certain individuals addressed this problem, but it is in the nature of societies that they remain conservative and traditional, and as the new Millennium dawned the overwhelming visual thrust of the LAS was still figurative, and remains so.

Sadly, Monica Smith died in her early '80's, after sending the Society her greetings for a wonderful 75th Anniversary in 1981 and keeping in touch from her nursing home, where she had received Judith Oyler bearing flowers from the Society. Her colleague Miss Elfrida Jahn, the Deputy Director of Libraries, Museums and Art Gallery from 1961, had become a member of the LAS.

1988 A Vintage Year

This was in many ways the best year of the decade with the Spring Exhibition back in the Usher and realising 30 sales, its highest ever total. The Funds were buoyant, thanks to these sales, and Max Marschner arranged yet another 'art to the people' exhibition of over 50 LAS exhibits, in Littlewood's store restaurant in May, with the theme 'All Our Gardens'. Noel Black, assisted by Nick Ellerby in a Schools liaison role, and backed by David Freeman the County's Art Advisor, pushed ahead with a scheme to attract talented school leavers into the Society as Associates so that they could have an outlet for any good art work they produced, when they were entering other professions and might therefore neglect a strong talent. Black felt it would also provide an ongoing source of recruitment to the Society.

Eric Doitch, *The Coconut Shy*

Echo managed some extra political capital out of the exhibition, featuring a photograph of Richard Harrison's pastel of a Mrs.Gina Adams, upset over the closure of the Citizens Advice Bureau. Harrison had worked from an Echo photograph. This vintage year closed with record sales of 38 works from the Autumn Show, giving an income of £467.

1989 The Nadin Effect

The Spring Exhibition had opened on June 10th at the Stamford Arts Centre, beautifully hung (as minutes record) by Nadin and Gill Ross. There were no sales, the doors were often found locked, the staff were disorganised over dates and could not provide stewards, and the whole event was discussed in a July committee meeting as the 'Stamford Post Mortem'. There had been problems in Stamford before, as Keith Roper could testify. Members pressed for the exhibition to return to the Usher and Wood assured them that wherever it could be housed, it would be. Nadin's new friend Eric Doitch had opened the Stamford Show. He was Viennese, had experienced a colourful early life with his family under threat from the Waffen S.S., and, following internment, had trained at Camberwell and the Royal College of Art. Teaching at Camberwell in the 1960's he went on to teach etching and lithography at Chelsea then in 1971 he and his wife Mary Fitzpayne came to Lincolnshire, eventually settling permanently in a fenland vicarage designed by Teulon. Mary had trained at Leeds, Central School, and the Royal College, and they had already exhibited at the Usher in 1983. They both acknowledge that they became involved with the LAS through Gill Nadin, whose work they found 'genuinely original' and whose intelligence and 'slight aloofness' echoed their own characters. 1989 was the year they both became full members of the Society.

The Embarassment of Readmission

Speed's swift removal of the names of Members defaulting on their subscriptions resulted in a number of the leading names having to reapply as Associates

The Autumn Exhibition (October 1st – November 6th) was Varcoe's last occasion as reviewer of LAS events, for he died in December aged only 62. he was able to sign off on a note that indicated the LAS had taken notice of Eyton and Coon the previous year: 'With such a gratifying standard it would be insidious to single out examples for individual comment…the usual plethora of flowers and sundry impressions of Lincoln Cathedral have largely given way to studies of a less hackneyed nature.'

The Opener was Philip Race, Chairman of the Heslam Trust, who became in this year a Vice-President of the Society along with Peter Brannan and Tony Bartl. The

before being required to present work for consideration as Full Members. This meant that even people like Pat Laing were jumping through these hoops in 1989, and it was not felt satisfactory. But Nadin acted again, this time proposing Speed, now anxious to retire as Treasurer, as an honorary Life Member. It was a popular suggestion, and it was agreed.

In October, a rare 'Emergency Meeting' of the Committee mulled over Nadin's threat to resign as Exhibitions Secretary as a result of a strong complaint from an unnamed Member whose work had been 'accepted but not placed'. Aligning herself with Wood, Nadin insisted that the maintenance of the highest standards was paramount, that Members should know they cannot raise complaints when procedures are so carefully spelled out to them, and so on. The committee calmed her down, and Noel Black recalls that many Members did not understand the rationale behind the selection process.

The exhibition for the Lincoln Festival was again organised by Marschner, this time in the form of small displays in some of Lincoln's public houses like the Turk's Head and the Victoria.

The Autumn Exhibition – Mixed Media

With 187 exhibits, the exhibition was opened by Geoffrey Wilson, already a living treasure of the Society, on October 14th. Bartl's supremacy in portraiture was challenged by Fenella Stoner who showed penetrating portraits of Peter Brannan and Dr. D. G. Stephenson. Gill Ross showed several floral pieces (and gave a talk on flower painting the following year), while Sue Hayward showed her mixed media work and a Ben Nicholson-like 'Watercolour of Four'. Roper's 'Cathedral from Southcliff' and Bartl's 'Springfields, Cambridgeshire' were outstanding, as were Coon's 'Rock Pool Studies', Laing's exciting abstract 'Helmsdale' and Judy Bowen-Jones's 'African Stripe', another multi-media work. Noel Black, now almost Chairman, showed versatility with

several 'Hedgescapes' in mixed media, while Alison Wilson showed her wax and dye on silk 'Butterfly', 'Iris' and 'Cineraria'. Asif Kamal shortly to be a Full Member, showed a gouache called 'Blue Hill' and Steve Wallhead showed four stoneware items. Doitch and Fitzpayne impressed by their craftsmanship and colour in oils of Freiston Shore (which Doitch made his own in an endless, atmospheric series) and 'Clowns and Dogs', a typically mysterious Fitzpayne exploring the world of people on the edge of society.

It was 'regretted' that the lack of space caused the non-exhibition of Helen Markham-Jones's 'RAF Cranwell'.

As the decade closed, it seemed the battle for quality had been won, while Speed's reforms had helped to put the LAS on a sound financial footing. The hopes of Williams, for variety in subject matter, size and medium, had been fulfilled, and Marschner had literally taken art to the people. The 1990's would see the resolution of membership issues, the deaths of outstanding members, and the first catalogues to use colour.

8

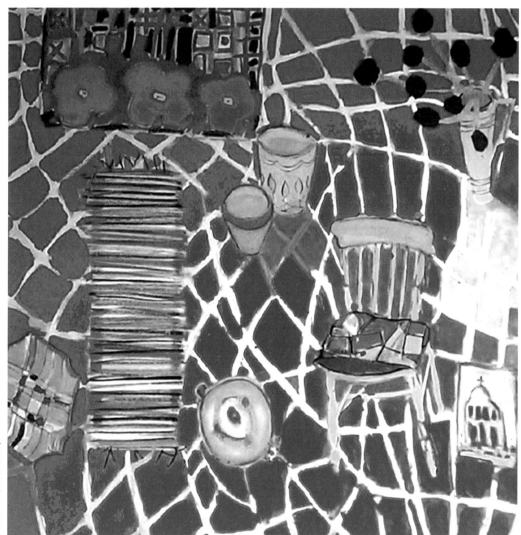

Janice Kok, *Red Quarry*

Claire Peasnall, *Banksia*

The Triumph of Professionalism

This would be a period of resolution, when Associate Memberships would cease after many years of argument, and the Society would regain its former name in the wake of local government reorganisation. The deaths of key members would result in memorial exhibitions and in some cases prizes in their memory. Professionalism would triumph, partly because of the ending of Associate Membership, taking with it the rather

mixed standard of works being submitted, and partly because presentation had become supremely important. By 2002 the Echo could describe the Society as 'Lincoln's very own Royal Academy', which in all but name, it has become.

1990 - Exhibitions Only

With the affable Noel Black in the Chair and Charles Speed entering his second decade as Treasurer, it was decided early in 1990 that for the time being and as a result of a very poor response from Members, activities other than the exhibitions would cease. In any case, Marschner had decided to bow out for a period in order to concentrate on other artistic projects, and Coon was not in the best of health at this time. Fenella Stoner assisted Speed by collecting subscriptions, and Pat Laing was proposed as Publicity Officer by Nadin. Doitch joined the committee, and Rosemary Lowery entered her second year as secretary.

Spring Becomes Late Summer

The usual LAS Spring Exhibition eventually materialised as a late summer show at Scunthorpe Museum from August 11th to September 9th. It was opened by Philip Grimes, Keeper of the Willoughby Memorial Gallery at Corby Glen, and contained 137 items, including Black's maquette for a 33ft steel and brass sculpture for Louth Methodist Church. Jean Parsons asked for £325 for a textile called 'The Bat', but P. A. Etherington was selling his screenprint of butterflies and Venetian masks for under £40.

...And the Autumn Exhibition Enters the New Year

Speed was concerned about the very late start of the Autumn Exhibition on December 8th and its termination 3 weeks into the New Year, explaining in a discussion paper how it created complications for the accounts. December 31st was no longer the best date for the end of the financial year and Speed suggested March 31st as more appropriate. But the winter weather created the

Roy Perry, *Somerby*

most immediate problem, for a snowbound Britain prevented the opener, Rigby Graham, from attending, and Tom Baker was prevailed upon at the last minute.

It was really a Christmas and New Year Show, full of the magical and the mysterious, though perhaps not purposely. Fitzpayne showed two lyrical and whimsical canvasses, 'Shah playing with Green Ball' and 'Shah playing with ribbon,' which displayed typical craftsmanship and finish. Bryan Page's large oil, 'Charnwood B5350 I' looked at first glance as though Keith Vaughan might have wandered into the Society, while Asif Kamal's expressionistic 'Seascape' tantalised with its symbolism. Mysterious abstraction was served

up by Hollinshead's 'Rocks and Water', but Roy Perry's 'Wold Road' brought Neo-Romanticism into the Usher. Bartl's watercolour portrait of Peter Brannan revealed the sitter's failing health and conveyed a sense of unease. Black presented four steel 'Woldscapes' and Wallhead contributed some stoneware. Perhaps most mysterious of all were Ellerby's exquisitely drawn 'Alice standing in her own tears' and 'Alice swimming in her own tears'.

A glimmer of the old Society was provided by Barrell's 'The Dogana' and 'Santa Maria della Salute', that touch of Venice which very few of the exhibitions had been without.

Richard Hatfield, *Wolds Landscape*

Sue Hayward Dies

A shocked and saddened committee heard on the morning of Saturday May 11th that Sue Hayward had died earlier that day in Lincoln St. Barnabas Hospice. Only 37 years old, she left two children. Gill Nadin, who was very close to her, conveyed the news and nobody present will ever forget the sadness which pervaded the meeting. She had fought her illness bravely from her wheelchair, and had been so enthusiastic and active in the Society. Fenella Stoner, with her nurse's training had helped to look after her. It was eventually decided to honour her memory with a Sue Hayward Award, to be a year's subscription to the Royal Academy which had been so close to her heart, as an encouragement to Associate Members.

The meeting struggled on to hear how the Spring Exhibition had gone, this year in Grantham at the Isaac Newton Centre. 82 exhibits had been chosen from 116 submissions, and with only 3 pictures sold, it was decided not to repeat the experience, for very few had taken an interest, costs amounted to £440, and Charles Speed had, according to Nadin, organised and dismantled the whole thing single-handed!

Autumn Flashpoint

At the invitation of Noel Black, the Autumn Exhibition Catalogue was sponsored by Lakeview Learning, whose Principal arrived at the Opening on October 19th finding it difficult to park his car. Distributing the catalogues was a very stressed Rosie Bradshaw, who reacted brusquely when Black asked for a copy to give to the Sponsor. Rigby Graham had this year been able to come over from Leicester to open the show but according to the sponsor he made no mention of Lakeview in his speech. Finally, although the Lakeview advert was prominent in the catalogue, there was an objection to the tiny acknowledgement of sponsorship on the back page – despite a request that it be discreet. As a result of a strong letter from the sponsor to Speed, Bradshaw resigned as membership Secretary and was comforted by Black, who shouldered all the blame. No disrespect was intended, and Bradshaw's concern at the time was simply to ensure that all Members received catalogues. She was simply doing her job.

The sponsored catalogue did, however, give a number of exhibitors the chance to have their work reproduced in colour. Quality and variety of media were evident. Black's virile steel sculptures, a series called 'Return to Meigle', contrasted with Peter Brannan's delicate, Whistlerian 'Still Life' in whites, greys and pinks, while Stoner contributed a spatially and psychologically teasing piece

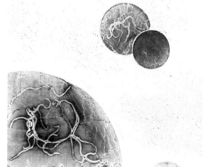

Kevin Wallhead, *Falling III*

Rex Chritchlow, *Chapel of St. Edmunds*

The judging of her Award would be done wherever possible by the Usher's Keeper. Black underlined the Society's debt to the Usher and its staff and said 'the surest way of losing the facilities is to allow our standards to fall.'

As the year closed, Laing was interviewed on Radio Nottingham about the Autumn Exhibition, and Tom Baker indicated that after 10 years as President he wished, at 80, to step aside and become vice-president so that his preferred choice, Peter Brannan, could succeed him. Stoner's letter to the Echo, suggesting that someone might write an independent review of the next Autumn Exhibition rather than just publish photographs, sadly met with no response, but Nadin wrote a very neat article on the Autumn Show for the Lincolnshire Life magazine.

1992 Buoyant Sales on Home Ground

Three exhibitions were mounted in 1992. A Winter Exhibition at Boston Arts Centre (January 2nd – February 5th) saw only 7 works sold, and only 26 of the 300 catalogues had been purchased by visitors – hardly a promising start, but things would improve with the Spring Exhibition (13th March – 26th April) back on home ground in the Usher. 16 of the 126 exhibits were sold. Catalogues with a new tactile quality had been designed by Paton, with covers which would serve for a number of exhibitions in order to reduce costs. Then came the Autumn Exhibition (14th November – 20th December) which realised almost 50 sales from 175 exhibits, gaining the Society £1060 in commission. Thanks to Asif Kamal's connection with Lincoln's hospitals, 17 works were purchased to adorn their corridors.

Pulped Iris Leaves, and a Mexican Hen

In recent years, the main suppliers of art materials in Lincoln, Gadsbys, had supplied prizes for the LAS exhibitions. But Ruddocks also have a large art department and donated a £50 art materials prize which the Opener of the Autumn Exhibition adjudicated. This

called 'December, and its cold outside'. Ralph Scott's watercolour, 'Winter Lake, Burton' was monumental in its balancing of reed masses, water and sky, while Bartl's portrait of Pat Bowers was riveting – and coolly sophisticated.

A Gracious AGM

Before stepping down for Roy Perry, Noel Black delivered a warm and typically gracious speech on October 19th paying a glowing tribute to Sue Hayward and stressing her concern to help and encourage others.

Leslie Stoneham, *Secret Form*

year it would be the other Bawden - Richard Bawden R.E., the printmaker, and son of Edward, who was faced with 175 exhibits, but only one stoneware pot, by Wallhead. All the usual subjects were there, but Judy Bowen-Jones showed constructions made from pulped straw, pulped iris leaves, grasses and scrap metal, while Jo Shaw showed batiks and Joan Perry showed a Mexican Hen on Thai silk, in gouache and pastel. Coon was continuing to relate music to art in his 'Ecstatic Song', an oil abstract on paper, and Tarttelin, coming and going from the LAS over the decades, showed 'Et in arcadia', 'Winter Sunset', and 'Baptism, Summer Feast'.

Peter Brannan, President

At the AGM on November 14th, David Morris was formally elected as the Membership and Subscriptions Secretary. He had computerised Members' records and had produced information sheets concerning the

Peter Moss, *Ceramic Form*

submission of works. Tom Baker was presented with a print of Lincoln by vice-president Stanley Barrell who thanked him for his work as President over the last decade. His successor Peter Brannan would preside over the biggest constitutional changes in the Society's history. His close friend Bartl had shown an oil portrait of the new President in the Autumn Exhibition. The first President of the Society since Warrener to be a practising artist, he was a very popular choice.

As the year closed, Paton presented a mounting and framing demonstration to a few interested members, and Speed entered 1993 on a buoyant note but no successor in sight, with a healthy balance of £2,355. The Society had 73 Full and 138 Associate Members.

1993 - The End of Associate Membership

For several years many Associate Members had been leaving the LAS because their submissions to exhibitions were never hung. Around 47 new members were enrolled each year, but almost the same number resigned by the end of the year. In 1993 only 47 of the 128 Associates had been members for 5 or more years. Morris had always been very concerned about this because of the Associate level accepting anyone regardless of their artistic ability. This inevitably sent a discouraging signal to artists of real achievement, who would be wary of joining a Society that did not discriminate. His ideas, and those of Speed, were the basis for committee discussions from March onwards. Roy Perry sent a letter to all Members based on Morris's and Speed's proposals in July. It stressed that the committee believed that the failure to attract and maintain artists of sufficient merit was an impediment to progress, and it proposed the ending of the designations 'Full Member' and 'Associate Member', so that there would only be Members, all with equal status. This had been Morris's main proposal, and if adopted, all artists seeking membership would have to submit a portfolio of no less than four recent works of a standard acceptable to the Management Committee. Perry commended

these changes to the membership, and everyone awaited the Extraordinary General Meeting set for November 13th.

Disappointment in Spring – Joy in Autumn

Scunthorpe Museum was again chosen as the venue for the Spring Exhibition, but there was only one sale and very few visitors. Only a contribution of £300 towards the cost of transport prevented a financial disaster. The show closed on May 16th. It was left to the Autumn Exhibition (November 14th – December 19th) to redeem the situation, and it did, with a healthy 37 sales. The Opener was Chris Sharp, an Independent Advertising Consultant who was born in Lincoln, attended Lincoln School of Art, and became Creative Director of a prestigious advertising agency in London. The Exhibition was given an excellent spread in the Echo with Dianne Davies, David Hollinshead and David Dennis standing by their paintings, and Gallery technician Chris Appleby adjusting the lighting. Nadin's comment included a remark which resonates even today: 'For my part I think it is nice to make sure that we are not seen as a backwater'. Hollinshead's 'Fiery Light' won the Judith Oyler Award, while Sue Banks won the Sue Hayward award, and Sue Blatherwick was awarded the Gadsby's Prize, which may have been a slight consolation, for her father had died in January and would be honoured with a small memorial exhibition by the Society.

202 exhibits found wall space, with Bowen-Jones's handmade paper Sculpture dangling from the ceiling like a Jacob's Ladder of Dead Sea Scrolls. Bartl showed 'Midnight Sea', 'North Sea', and 'Tidal Wave', while Paton showed 'Suffolk Marshes', 'Mudflats at Blythborough' and 'Rain clouds'. Heather Muddiman, always pushing the boundaries of art, contributed 'Cloud Hidden Destination Unknown', a multi-media print. Noel Brannan showed his industrial Leicestershire subjects, Lowery showed a charcoal of 'Cabbages' and Gill Ross devoted her monoprints to Celtic Myths and magic. Sam Scorer weighed in for the architects with a model for Holy Trinity Church in Louth, together with a concept sketch.

Resolved!

Meanwhile the AGM of November 13th made two historic resolutions:

That the Society reverts to its former name, and with effect from April 1st 1994 will be called the Lincolnshire Artists' Society.

Former designations of Membership would cease, leaving everyone as Members. There would however be Honorary Life Members, to include all Presidents and Vice Presidents ex-officio, otherwise to be awarded as a gesture of esteem and nominated for a majority vote at the AGM. The category of Friends would be for supporters of the Society with no desire to exhibit.

1994 A Vibrant New Logo

David Paton's new logo for the re-named Society achieved a remarkably vivid optical effect reminiscent of landscape and light. It replaced Hollinshead's familiar non-geometrical meditation on the same theme, and suggested a new dawn, of equal opportunity. At first, though, opportunities to exhibit were not taken, and after discussion, Keith Roper and his committee decided that the Society's reputation was not enhanced when so few of the Members submitted for the Spring Exhibition. The '94 Spring Exhibition had been at the South Holland Centre, Spalding (May 3rd – 30th). No grant had been available and only 4 works had been sold. It was decided to hold Spring Exhibitions only when venues and conditions did justice to the Society. Perhaps Rosemary Lowery was having a joke when she recorded Judy Bowen-Jones's name in the committee as 'J. Bowes-Lyon', or perhaps it was just tiredness, but she gave notice that she would be retiring as Secretary, not because of the work, but because she had 'missed so many meetings'. She had willingly done the job for six years, assisted behind the scenes by Speed, and had been successful in having her farm scenes (such as 'Sow and Litter') hung in LAS exhibitions even when she was an Associate Member a decade earlier.

Enter Peter Moss……and farewell to two much loved members

The Autumn Exhibition (November 19th – December 18th) contained exactly 200 exhibits but only two sculptures, if Echo photographer Roy Ealdon's papier mache 'Come to the Circus' and 'Mermaid Breakfast' could be so termed. Peter Moss, the retiring Vice-Principal of the Lincoln College of Art and a distinguished ceramic sculptor, opened the show, although he did not exhibit any work with the LAS until 1998. Apart from the many works betraying exotic holiday venues, there were visual explorations in series such as Jenny Hammerton's 'Shed and Fields', Jackie Lee's 'Stones - I-IV' and somewhat astonishingly, Muddiman's 'Menstrual' I to III etchings. Fitzpayne introduced a sinister note with two Punch and Judy drawings while Ross-Kelsey continued in mystical vein with 'Cosmos', 'Dawn' and 'Mystical Forms'. All the usual names were exhibiting apart from the Marschners, Bartl, and one who would never exhibit again, for Mary Dudding, perhaps the most highly-strung member the Society has ever had, was dead. Over the years, other Full Members had seen their work rejected on several occasions, but she took rejection very personally and pursued those she felt were responsible. Yet she could be charming, forgiving and appreciative. She was the last of the old members residing in the shadow of the Cathedral. And another blow fell as the year ended, when having exhibited as usual in the Autumn Exhibition, Peter Brannan died at the age of 68. Successful and highly esteemed in London, and a Member of the Royal Society of British Artists since 1960, he reserved his greatest commitment and affection for Lincolnshire and the LAS, as did hid father and brother. As Eric Newton said of this much loved man, he was to Newark what Utrillo had been to Montmartre, and, like Boudin, 'he watched the grey-green sea lashed by cold winds under a grey sky'. His family thought of him as Mozart to Noel's Beethoven - a most apt comparison. He would be commemorated at the Usher and at the Goldmark Gallery in Uppingham, and will always remain one of Lincolnshire's finest painters.

Rosemary Lowery, *Landrace X Large White*

1995 A Lean Year

The Society was unable to find a suitable venue for the Spring Exhibition, which did not take place. The breathing-space had symbolic importance, for the idea for such exhibitions had been Peter Brannan's, even if the LAS also saw them as an opportunity for the Associate members to 'get value for money' from their subscriptions by doubling the opportunity to submit works.

The Autumn Exhibition (November 4th to December 17th)

A poignant tribute to Peter Brannan appeared without words on the cover of the catalogues, and in monochrome. Bartl's haunting study of his friend had the eyes looking slightly beyond the viewer, dark eyes now extinguished forever. The exhibition by contrast glowed with life and health, and in the Echo on November 18th Morris declared that 'traditional styles are the most popular.' Figurative work and traditional landscapes dominated but Ross-Kelsey contributed four acrylic abstracts exploring blue and yellow, and Morris obliged in the now rather token sculpture section, with resin and cement-fondue portraits of young children. Ellerby was back with another stunning portrait of 'Alice', and Elaine James of Swaton, an enthusiastic painter of sports people in action, contributed 'Fast Bowlers'. Muddiman, moving on from her 'Menstrual' etchings, showed

Peter Moss, *Ceramic Form*

'Ecology', 'Bamboo' and 'Root'. Joan lock was still exploring her conservatory in superb lino-prints while Roper and Hollinshead were on top form with pastels of brooding landscapes. The prices also drew the eye. Frank Marston, a Camberwell-trained Member, who would become the Society's Secretary in 1999, was asking £1250 for an oil of 'Yew Tree Farm, Coniston', while works by Doitch and Fitzpayne were getting on for £1000. Members had felt for some time that prices charged in Lincoln were far too low and did not reflect the Society's status. That was now changing. Tim Couldwell won the Sue Hayward Award for a large figure study.

At the AGM, Roper handed over the Chairmanship to Paton. With his friend Morris as Secretary for the second time and Speed in his 16th year as Treasurer, the Society was about to elect a natural successor to Brannan as President – Geoffrey Wilson. Sadly, because of a heart problem, Wilson felt he could not continue in the role and had to step down, creating a challenge for the committee. That challenge was met and resolved in 1997.

1996 Gill Nadin Dies

David Morris began a New Year message to Members with the promise of a very busy year, but barely three weeks later, Gill Nadin died, in her late '60's. Her obituary in the Echo mentioned how she had achieved 'new and exciting' standards for the Open College of Arts, of which she was a tutor. Max Marschner paid eloquent tribute:

> *"Gill was very grand, very even-handed. A wonderful person, she transformed the mundane."*

There would be many more tributes and a Society prize in her name, and perhaps best of all, the Nadin Group. Jackie Lee, Jenny Hammerton and other students in Nadin's Open College Group did not want things to end once their course had ended, so Nadin suggested they hire a room in the WEA on Beaumont Fee. Every Wednesday night they met for guidance and criticism, and when she died it seemed natural that the group should call itself the Nadin Group. Still thriving today, it holds exhibitions and keeps the name alive.

The Spring Exhibition returned to the Usher between March 2nd and March 24th. Sensibly, Morris redefined the nature of submissions as 'restricted to works on paper framed under glass.' 110 exhibits realised 12 sales, Hollinshead selling three pastels and Ellerby a gum print of Louth Church. Morris sold two of his four 'Lincoln' oils, while Sue Blatherwick's landscapes were made from 'natural and un-natural found materials and tissue paper'. There was no limit to what could be put on paper under glass!

Then came the Summer Exhibition, suggested and run by English Heritage who had originally contacted Nadin in 1994. The Alnwick Tower in the ruins of Lincoln's Old Bishop's Palace was an intriguing venue, but sadly, 11 works by Roper, Barrell and Richard Harrison were stolen and the show had to be closed down. Amazingly, all the paintings were recovered subsequently, in an auction room in Scotland!

The Autumn Exhibition included a 17-work tribute to Nadin, selected by Morris and Paton. Peter Williams made a welcome return visit to open the show and included references to the Society's history in his speech. Only 126 works were selected. Ross-Kelsey had four acrylic ink pieces called 'Broken Edge'. Micheal Logan showed four etchings with aquatint including 'Front and Best Seat in the Bus'.

Leslie Stoneham had been exploring Lincoln Market, while Ellerby and Allen Smith had clearly been to St. Ives. The only sculptural item was Marston's 'Green Man', cast from magnesium limestone and the only oddity was the restoration of the correct spelling of Sidney Wright's name, which had appeared as 'Sydney' in many other catalogues. And on the cover was a Nadin, an etching of the tools of her trade, called 'Worktable – Still life'. The Society had celebrated its 90th year, and it seems likely that although, because of the inactive years of the First World War, the show was not itself the 90th, this numbering had been adopted in order to prevent confusion. A consultation of the Society's first minute book will confirm that there were no exhibitions during that war.

Fenella Stoner, *Spaced Out*

1995 A Successor to Charles Speed

Some time in 1995, Charles Speed had at last been able to retire as the most thorough treasurer the LAS had had to date. Micheal Logan, a committee member and printmaker, took the job on for two years until the committee appointed a retired teacher who had been head of the Adult Education Service in Lincoln for many years - John Maddison. Speed slipped away quietly, albeit with the gratitude of a society he had brought back from the financial brink. A highly regarded watercolourist, Speed continued to exhibit before leaving Lincoln for his retirement proper. He valued the friendships he had made in the LAS, and they regarded him as the authority on the constitution which he had done so much to shape.

Everything Happens in Threes

The Autumn Exhibition ran from November 16th – December 21st. The Echo's photo article carried a very brief text which highlighted a tribute exhibition to Bartl, with 16 works shown alongside the 155 exhibits in the

Cilla Chapman, *Grids II: Garden*

two project drawings and Scorer showing an architectural model of no. 1 Westwood Avenue, Leeds. Both men showed paintings on other subjects. Speed, Horner, Roper, Fitzpayne and Doitch were all singled out in the Echo article, Roper's pastel of the 'Lincoln University Site' no doubt creating a topical flurry. Otherwise, members were exhibiting in threes. Stoner presented three 'Reveries in Hues' in oil, M. D. Hargreaves had three pastels of 'Tree Pruning', Muddiman challenged yet again with three drypoints called 'Have You Seen The Emperor's New Clothes?', and Paton showed three watercolours of Strath Dionard. Louise Smith had three 'Ochre Crosses' and Jacky Lee decided on two 'Recollections' and a 'Transition'. Marston, fluent in carving as in printmaking and painting, presented his 'Roman Youth' in Ketton Oolite limestone, and 'Winter Trees at Sunset', a wood-engraving for a very attractive £60. No LAS Autumn Show seemed complete without Ellerby's 'Alice' who may prove to have been the Society's most featured girl, but Ellerby was already proving to be a fine landscapist, as future exhibitions would reveal.

The Bartl Touch

'The Society recognises the enormous contribution that Tony Bartl has made to art education within the County and his support of the Society over many years. Both his teaching and his painting have been a source of inspiration to many…'

Thus ran the printed introduction to the Master's latest appearance. The Midas of the portrait, Bartl had now immortalised another four sitters – Peter Moss, Cash Scorer, Dr. Jenny Eremin, and Mrs. Broadbent. His self-portrait of 1947 in oil was there, too, as was a pencil study for his portrait of John Piper. The longer you looked, the more you were seduced. Bartl went beyond likeness to touch the essence, in portraits, landscapes, and even in an abstract of a 'Friction Weld'. And there was a lot more to come…

main exhibition, and also mentioned the very high price attached to a watercolour called 'The Secret Garden' by Gillian Beale - £1,500. Architecture integrated itself seamlessly into this show, with Rex Critchlow showing

Jacky Lee, *Cave I*

Meanwhile the talk was all of a new President, almost a year after Wilson stepped down. Paton and Morris, on behalf of the committee, approached Peter Moss, not least because he had given an inspirational speech on the importance of drawing when he opened the 1994 Autumn Exhibition. Moss accepted.

David Paton handed on the Chairmanship to Gill Ross-Kelsey who had originally joined the LAS from Grimsby to see whether she could get a picture in the Annual Exhibition because of the Society's reputation. She was

one of those who were pleased to see the end of Associate Membership, and found the new system 'much fairer'.

1998

Gill Ross-Kelsey made a far-reaching decision when she invited artist and teacher Cilla Chapman to join the LAS in 1998. Chapman was invited straight onto the committee because of her experience in higher education. While living in Chiswick she had known several Royal Academicians in the area and had been

Carol Butler, *Second Hand Roses*

Bartl, Brannan and Nadin – Lengthening Shadows

The Usher hosted a nine week exhibition of the works of Bartl, Peter Brannan and Nadin, from August 31st in effect, this show proposed and celebrated the three giants of the LAS. At first, Bartl was not sure it would be a good idea to have the show, since both of the others had died, but he responded to the Echo's interviewer, saying that Nadin and Brannan had been great friends of his, and adding that 'Peter visited every week and we talked about painting.' The article carried a photograph of Bartl and spoke of 'these eminent artists'. The trio were linked, too, in their outspoken aversion to 'Sunday painters', an aversion which in Nadin's case ran deeply enough for her to invent a new committee post in order to keep a retiring professional on the committee so that no 'Sunday painters' could occupy the vacancy! Bartl was unwell at the Opening, and died the day before Christmas Eve.

A Fitting Farewell for Tony Bartl

The funeral had to be held in the New Year. As Tony's wife, Sheila, said, even undertakers have holidays. She and Tony had been together ever since they met at the Lincoln Art School where she was a student and he the charismatic and handsome new lecturer. The ceremony was not a service, for Tony was an atheist, and Czech music was played between tributes, two of which were from Peter Moss and the distinguished potter Gordon Baldwin, who had himself trained under Tony. Gordon and his painter wife Nancy had a brief membership of the LAS, but found it physically impossible to commit to regular involvement. Thus passed the most admired and revered artist in the Society's history. Not everyone warmed to his work, and many critics passed over it, while Anthony Eyton disliked it, but Bartl had earned a lasting place in 20th century English art, and there are signs that his reputation will grow.

Hillier's Choice, Howard's Return

The 1998 Annual Exhibition was doubly blessed in having Ken Howard yet again as its Opener, and

head of art at two schools. Voted Vice-Chairman of the LAS shortly after her arrival onto the committee, she would eventually revolutionise the way the committee dealt with business. Her own art dealt with relational politics and she worked in grid patterns inspired by Mondrian, Schwitters and Turner.

Frank Marston, *Nude*

distinguished local painter Graham Hillier as the invited selector of his own choice of works for Gallery V. Claire Peasnall had approached Hillier on behalf of the committee, and he decided to base his choices on his own passion for landscapes and places. A magnificent display of ceramics added to the distinction of this show, for Peter Moss contributed four dramatic sculptured ceramics replete with mystical and multi-cultural references, and Bob Blatherwick's pots occupied two cases in a memorial tribute exhibition. 'Samurai's Kimono' was in effect Moss's calling card as the new

President, and he continued to produce exquisitely glazed variants on this strong shape. As a member, he showed three further ceramics in a show which featured 139 exhibits.

Stafford Critchlow, Rex's son, made a distinguished debut, for Hillier chose his 'Gorbio' watercolour and 'The Poetics of Space',a charcoal and collage piece. Coincidentally, there were several carps in this show, for Brian Mason showed 'a visit to a Carp Pond' (also chosen by Hillier) and a new Member Hai Shuey Yeung

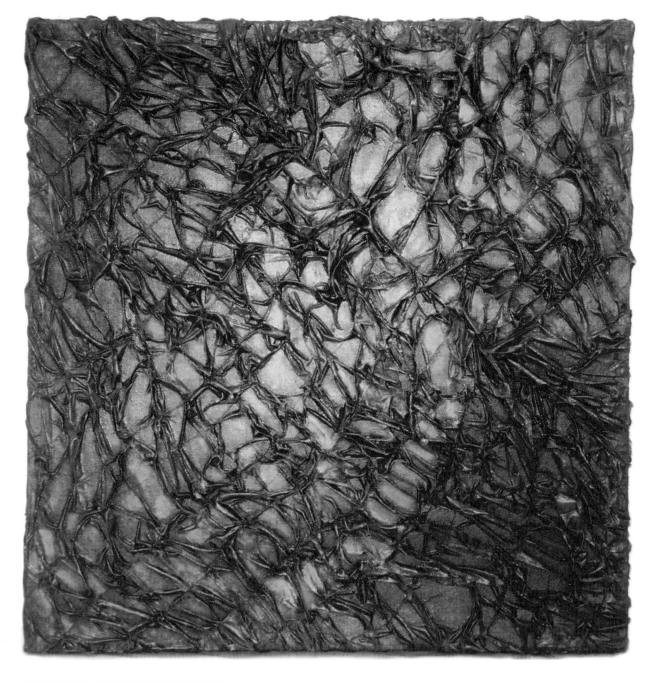

Jenny Hammerton, *Untitled (Mixed Media on Canvas)*

Sue Blatherwick, *Time and Tide, 1991*

showed 'Swimming Carp' in two watercolours, asking £1500 for one of them. Yeung was a Chinese restaurant owner in Grimsby and, not surprisingly, the media latched on, with the Grimsby press showing him with one of his landscapes. Bartl showed oil portraits of Carol Butler and her husband Paul, and Hillier featured one of Carol. The Echo featured a photograph of Ken Howard smiling in front of Ken Lee's 'Chatsworth House' (watercolour and ink) which won the Stanley Barrell Prize for watercolour and the Gill Nadin prize for the President's Choice of a drawing in any medium. Without

in any way detracting from Lee's achievement, Howard afterwards told Carol Butler that his inclination had been to award the Barrell Prize to Bartl's portrait of her, but he had to stick to the watercolours.

Let's Face it!

The Autumn Exhibition 1999 (November 28th – December 19th) explored the idea of facing things and many artists incorporated 'Face it' into their titles. Marian Taylor's pen and wash drawing carried the most humorous title: 'Face it – He's Still There'. But Graham

Lewington's oil was called 'Work (Face it)', Ellerby's photograph 'Angel's Head (Face it)' and Ken Lee decided to face everything with 'Face it –Life', 'Face it –Death' and 'Strait Face it'. Fitzpayne joined in with 'Face to Face'. M. A. Addison determined to be included with '8 faces' in pencil, and Michael Logan contributed 'Face it: a Conservative View'.

Moss's ceramics were now an established feature of the exhibitions and this year he explored ideas around tearing and drawing. Roper was consolidating his position as the visual poet of Nocton while Doitch was taking a break from his beloved Freiston Shore with 'Footballers' and 'the Wrestling Bout'. Yeung was in again with one carp study and two 'water and oil' studies called 'Space 49' and 'Space 1998'. Ross-Kelsey showed a series called 'Summer Flowers', in acrylic monoprints, and Butler showed lilies and 'Second Hand Roses'. Jenifer Critchlow appeared for the LAS's exhibiting family of architects with a study of the 'Arabella Aufrere Temple' and 'Brocklesby Mausoleum'. Venice belonged to Sarah Webb this year, but Laing had clearly been on the Italian Riviera. Kevin Wallhead contributed three glass and copper pieces called 'Darkside', 'Reclining Figure' and 'Sit with Me'.

Ben Levene RA opened the show, chatted individually with the artists, and was very warmly received.

2000 An Accolade for the Millenium

Fenella Stoner succeeded Ross-Kelsey as Chairman at a time when there were more professionals in the LAS than ever before. She achieved a degree in Fine Art partly in order to feel that she could hold her own alongside Nadin, but she had been a notable founder of art groups, starting one at Branston College which lasted 17 years, taking on the Nadin Group, and organising figure-drawing sessions at the Usher. Laing, the Marschners and Dennis Valentine took part in notable exhibitions held at Branston. Her Chairmanship was marked by her belief that everyone, regardless of age or status, should be nurtured in the Society, at a time when young exhibitors were being encouraged. This was good for the Society, but Stoner felt that the young would inevitably move on, and that commitment to the workings and the idea of the Society was usually shown by the more mature Members. Familiar names who had been around for decades might now have only one work selected for the Autumn Exhibition, or none, instead of their usual quota of four. It was perhaps inevitable, and as Stoner said, part of her role was 'keeping the peace' in a period of creative tension between young and old.

Erich Doitch dies June 7th 2000

The latest loss to the Society and the wider art world came with Doitch's death. The Freiston shore had lost its visual poet and perhaps its greatest lover, and David Buckman, writing his Obituary for the Independent, said 'Doitch's name is not as well-known as it should be.' Like Bartl, he felt no commercial drive and lacked a London outlet, but the quality of his work will endure, as will the life in his paintwork, and the joyful colours of the Fairgrounds he and his wife had always loved.

But the Society's own Carousel had to keep moving, despite sad departures which included Paton's retirement from the Committee after almost continuous service since 1965. The LAS showed its appreciation and gratitude for his 'enormous contribution' by mounting a representative show of his work alongside an Autumn Exhibition, opened this year by John Ward CBE RA, Stoner's choice and a distinguished portraitist. Commending the exhibition very highly, he said that it was superior to work on show in London, echoing the opinions of the 1950's. Lady Monson, one of the Society's Vice Presidents, had commissioned Ward to paint her children, and was willing to loan his preparatory drawings to the Usher but the staff felt unable to guarantee their security. Ward, though hard of hearing, enjoyed his day and commended artworks which were simple and direct, rather than pretentious and overly serious.

Ken Lee, *War Memorial, Paddington Station*

Maggie Dean, *Tetney Lock First Frost*

affection as a result. His assistants had also helped the LAS to hold all manner of events in the gallery, and Judith Robinson and Ros Thomas had been responsible for the Bartl, Brannan and Nadin show, whose catalogue reminded the public of the close relationship between J. D. Wheeldon and Sons as framers and exhibitors of so many LAS artists, and the Usher. Julie Allsop came from Gainsborough Old Hall to take over from Wood, her special interest being in Design history.

The Open Approach...and some eminent lecturers

The Society was becoming more publicity-conscious at this time and Claire Peasnall, a superb botanical watercolourist, was appointed to deal with publicity and events such as lectures. As well as her other qualifications, she had recently studied at the Courtauld Institute, exhibited a number of watercolours of such subjects as 'Cowslips', 'Indian Balsam' and 'Red Hot Pokers', and before she left Lincolnshire in 2002, an impressive array of Usher workshops and guest lectures had been organised with the support of the City and County Councils and East Midlands Arts. Jennifer Fletcher of the Courtauld spoke on 'Venetian Renaissance Collectors', Timothy Hyman spoke on Bonnard and Stanley Spencer, and Professor Germaine Greer presented a taste of one her books, about the Male Nude in European Art, called 'The Boy, The Boy'. In 2004, Peter Williams came again to talk to the Society about the Turner Prize. It was a provocative evening and Williams, recovering from 'flu, collapsed at the end, to be rushed to hospital! Fortunately, he recovered.

Meanwhile, on the back of each catalogue, a tempting cross-section of the Society's activities was set out in a welcoming paragraph.

2001

With the arrival of the Sam Scorer Gallery on Drury Lane the opportunity at last presented itself for an exhibition of 'Large Works', and this year some 40 members were able to contribute in sizes that had often been 'accepted

Meanwhile, August 2000 had seen a notable departure. Richard Wood, in charge of the Usher for 30 years, departed for Anglesey Abbey in Cambridgeshire, where he would be in charge, and working for the National Trust. The Usher Gallery Trust had been his brainchild, an entirely independent venture outside the control of the County Council, which would benefit the collections within the Usher. His enthusiasms had been in the heritage and research areas. A large gathering in the Usher bade farewell to the man who had 'fought the LAS's corner' for so long and had been held in great but not hung' at the Annual Usher shows. The Society was now getting used to a Summer Show at the Usher, and this year's exhibition was accompanied by a series of workshops and lectures by members, and a tribute exhibition for Eric Doitch, whose carousel painting provided probably the most colourful catalogue cover so far. Chapman was photographed against her multi-layered grid-based works which seem to emanate light and movement. She told the Echo 'there is such a range of work in this Society and the Exhibition is really like the Royal Academy Show, only in Lincoln.' Richard Hatfield undertook the hanging in three of the Usher's galleries including the Curtois Wing. 'To astounding effect, the contemporary and the traditional have been combined,' said Echo reporter Helen Greener. Hatfield remarked on the process of putting an exhibition together like a big jigsaw. 'It isn't about individual pieces alone, but about the building of an overall artistic experience.' It seemed that the work done by Williams and Wood towards realising that 'overall artistic experience', rather than a hotch potch of too many works, had borne fruit with the New Millenium. Julie Allsop opened the exhibition.

The Last of the Brannans

In August, Noel Brannan (1921-2001) died. Bartl had taught him at Lincoln and they had been firm friends. Noel's depiction of the industrial Midlands and the more humdrum areas of cities like Bath and Blackpool were steeped in atmosphere and he could make even a gas tank look good. His seeming spontaneity and sweeping strokes were the ideal complement to his younger brother's quiet precision, but his work was no less considered.

2002

Peter Moss opened the Summer Show, which again filled the usual two upstairs galleries and the Curtois Wing, with over 175 exhibits. Richard Hatfield once again arranged the hanging sequence and the Echo delivered a positive verdict: 'Painters, sculptors and printmakers from all over the County have their work on

Jill Marschner, *Child With Cat*

display at Lincoln's own Royal Academy.' The article mentioned the 'challenging abstract work by Leslie Stoneham' and said that 'images of the Lincolnshire landscape rubbed shoulders with the vibrant colours of Africa and dark, downtown Los Angeles.' It mentioned that Richard Devereux was holding a lecture entitled 'Art, Spirit, Cosmos' on November 20th, and that Alison Read would be running a wildlife-themed printmaking workshop. The Echo's coverage was probably the strongest ever seen, with Graham Lewinton and his large 'Union Jack' of sizzling textures ablaze for the main article, plus a 'gallery' of work on two inner pages.

Cilla Chapman, the new Chairman, put forward a plan to rationalise the agendas of the committee and place the Society on a firmer financial footing, looking firstly at its stated objectives. She felt that the forthcoming Centenary would be better prepared for if a series of sub-committees, dealing with aspects like finance and publicity, were set up. At first the committee feared that this would increase their workload, but after each sub-committee had reported back to the Management Committee it was found that the agenda could be reduced from 20 items to something like seven. This mirrored Chapman's 'grids' in that the activity in each square was ultimately unified by the whole.

From October 5th to November 4th, The Muriel Barker Gallery at Grimsby hosted 106 exhibits by LAS Members in an Autumn Exhibition of Small Works. The North East Lincolnshire Council generously supported this venture by funding the catalogue, but there were not many sales.

Finally for 2002, the death of the highly regarded potter Steve Wallhead was recorded.

2003 Taking the Long View on Gardens

Chapman had invited her friend Martin Postle to open the Annual Exhibition this year. A curator at Tate Britain, author of the 'Art of the Garden' and creator of Tate Britain's exhibition on that theme, Postle came to Lincoln the year before the bicentenary of the Royal Horticultural Society so that the LAS could get to work on a gardens theme for the 2004 Annual Exhibition. In the absence of other LAS exhibitions in 2003 (because no suitable venues could be found and there were often problems with disabled access). Members concentrated their efforts on the Usher show. Between May 31st and August 17th, 145 exhibits greeted the visitors and life-drawing and portrait painting workshops were held in the Curtois Wing.

Roy Ealdon, *Thoroughly Modern Dame (Papier Maché)*

Venice Again...and Las Palmas

Ken Lee's portrait of Sam Scorer in ink and watercolour was a wonderful demonstration of his Hokusai-like powers of distillation and emphasis. 3-dimensional work was plentiful and ranged from Moss's ceramics in precious metal lustres, through Kevin Wallhead's 'Solar Storm' in glass and copper, to Caroline Matthaei's Limewood Copper and Brass sculptures. But while Max

Marschner's etchings concentrated on France, almost everyone else went for Venice (or in Jill Marschner's case, Genoa at night). Leading the Venetian stakes was David Morris with four watercolours, but that other committed Venetian, Edith Cook, showed a 'Grand Canal', Michael Gibson showed 'Venice' in mixed media and Hollinshead showed a pastel of 'Strolling Dog, Venice'. Jean Dixon shot off to Las Palmas and produced an oil of 'Las Palmas from the Mountains'. Roper continued his dramatic pastel surveys of Lincolnshire and the Solent, and Jill Carter had a gouache called 'Catching Lincolnshire Light'.

Laing on the Edge

The most interesting title proved, in hindsight, to be Patricia Laing's 'The Edge', an acrylic. Sadly she was herself on the edge of life, and passed away aged 80, in 2004. Her dramatic paintings with their instinctive strong designs had been a feature of LAS shows for decades. Her committee work and commitment to the Society were exemplary, and she became synonymous with the Blakeney area. She had once had a Design business on Steep Hill, and she even taught driving. A diminutive figure, she looked dramatic in dark glasses, and she was a familiar sight in the Cathedral precincts where she and her doctor husband lived.

2004 It's all in the Undergrowth

Problems over the suitability of venues continued, so once again there were no exhibitions other than the Annual at the Usher. One exciting project materialised when Laraine Cooper of the Friary Learning Centre asked Peter Moss to work with her students on a very tactile ceramics-based project, which soon had youngsters with visual and aural impairments making all sorts of terra-cotta, tiled and ink-drawn products, which are now displayed or used in the Centre. Decorative panels, money boxes, wall sequences or models, involving subjects like 'Faces' or the four seasons, were completed to a very high standard. Also, some of Moss's ceramics were displayed in the Reception area.

Meanwhile, Cilla Chapman had experienced the first three year Chairmanship. Previously, the Chairman became 'Immediate Past Chairman' for two years, but this was felt to be unhelpful, and yet again David Morris came up with the idea of a three year term, so that instead of serving for the usual two, then lingering on for two further years, a Chairman would be able to develop

his or her ideas for the Society more freely. Carol Butler, who succeeded Chapman, decided to devote herself to the organisation of events which would culminate in the Centenary in 2006. Initially, like so many other Members, she had been inspired and spurred on by Gill Nadin to concentrate solely on her art, and she went on to win major prizes for portraiture. She is also interested in the development of the Friends of the Society.

David Paton opened the 2004 Annual Exhibition which began on September 18th at the Usher. Its theme was 'The Garden' and in this 'Year of the Garden', English Nature had devised a competition which required the representation of a good place in the garden for wildlife. Alison Wilson, without intending her work as an entry, won it with her batik of 'undergrowth'. There was another surprise, too, for Sheila Bartl could find no portraits of humans worthy of the Bartl Prize for Portraiture, and decided finally to award it to one of Fenella Stoner's cats!

2005 '300x300'

The first event of the year took place at Richard Hatfield's Ropewalk Gallery at Barton-on-Humber from February 19th to April 3rd. Members had to submit work restricted to the size of 300 x 300mm, including 3D work, and the challenge was met and enjoyed. The show tempted several visitors to enquire about joining the Society. Maggie Dean, the current Membership Secretary, said she had sent forms to several people, and reported in committee that there were now almost 140 Members, of whom about 100 are practising artists.

The Summer Exhibition (July 16th – September 25th) was opened by Jo Volley, artist and senior lecturer at the Slade. She singled out some of the Prizewinning works and admired Ellerby's landscapes. 136 exhibits included several three-dimensional works including Moss's multi-fired ceramics, Ashi Marwaha's silver dishes and Janice Kok's 'Allegory of Abundance: Horn of Plenty', which won the Sue Hayward Award for the most progressive work, and was chosen by the new Usher Keeper, Jeremy Webster, who had succeeded Julie Allsop in 2002. The Nadin Prize, sponsored by the Nadin Group, went to Robert Machan's oil 'High Street' as the most outstanding drawing in any media, and the Bartl portraiture prize was won by Neil Helyard for 'Gypsy Girl'. Jacky Lee's 'Entrance 11', a dramatic abstract oil painting, was chosen for the Society of Architect's Prize for the most architectural painting. Marschner's etchings of 'Souvenir – 263 Prinsengracht' and 'Dymchurch – Homage to Paul Nash' were steeped in atmosphere, as was Allen Smith's oil 'Hazy Day in Venice'. The show was superbly hung and held something for everyone whether it was the richly coloured humour of Maggie Dean's 'Mrs. Ed and Moppet Dawson', or Carol Butler's mysterious abstract 'Secrets'.

A Sketching Trip to Cambridge and Adventures in the Picture Trade

On Friday 22nd July, Society members joined artists from North Lincolnshire on a coach trip to Cambridge organised by Rex Critchlow, whose informed and cheerful descriptions of architectural highlights en route contributed to a very successful event. The landscape painter Barry Carter, a Member of LAS for 10 years, went with his artist wife Jill, and said how he valued their membership as a means to exhibit work and to visit other places. Rex Critchlow conducted a survey on preferred choices of venues for future sketching outings.

Finally in this year of intense preparation for the Society's Centenary, Mike Goldmark, director of the Goldmark Gallery at Uppingham, gave this year's talk on October 20th in the Usher. It was called 'Adventures in the Picture Trade'. The Goldmark Gallery represents Noel and Peter Brannan, and held superb retrospective exhibitions of their work shortly after their deaths.

Whither the Society?

Peter Moss had already presided over a vast improvement in the LAS's financial position and shortly after becoming President he posed the question 'Whither the Society?' to an audience of Members at the Usher. Moss feels that part of his role is to challenge and 'shake-up' the attitudes and practices in the Society and, as he says, he has no axes to grind. Ken Lee was one of those who were impressed by Moss's speech. One of the most revered members of the Society, he can see the temptation to try to encourage or embrace works on video, performance or installation.

Already the LAS has embraced photography, thanks in large measure to David Paton, but Lee feels that the Society will thrive if it welcomes works which require no technologically elaborate equipment and are not dependent on other people. He sees the current practitioners of such forms eventually 'succumbing to atavism' and returning to the simple and direct art forms. And he believes that they will then join the Society. These are wise thoughts from an artist whose work looks more youthful than that of many teenagers.

Younger members continue to be encouraged and the LAS hopes to attract graduates or students from Lincoln's University, which recently helped two of the LAS's newer members to achieve higher degrees in Fine Art. Jenny Hammerton's and Janice Kok' are proud to be members, and Janice Kok feels that the Society is 'like an artists' collective, a source of friendship, inspiration and common spirit'. While Hammerton's work is concerned with 'order and chance' and is based partly on the Lincolnshire landscape, Kok's work seems to stem from issues, and was powerfully described in a recent review by Ken Lee in which he said that her painting 'Occupation II', *came off the wall at 100 miles an hour'*.

After leaving Lincoln College of Art and before moving to London, Catherine Howells was one of the youngest members ever to serve on the committee, and the Society was sorry to lose her. A prize-winner in 2004, she is a very talented photographer.

Criteria for the Selection of Works and the Election of New Members

In the Foreword of the Ferens Winter Exhibition in 2002, Lucien Cooper, one of the exhibitions selectors, spelled out what was being looked for in a work of art, and this inspired the LAS exhibition committee in March 2002 who agreed that his statement reflected the main points to consider when selecting works for exhibition or electing new Members. They added that presentation was also very important. Cooper's points were:

- Original use of materials
- Fresh subject matter
- Energy
- Joy in production
- Technical competence
- Imaginative composition
- 'Inventiveness' – something not seen before, something new.

Currently, the entire committee including President and Vice-Presidents vote on new members' work and work to be included in exhibitions, with the addition of one member of the Usher staff present at exhibition selections. For the Centenary, the LAS may try a new formula for the selection committee, of just four committee members plus one member of the Usher Staff plus one invited selector. Richard Hatfield, the Hon. Secretary, is responsible for the hanging, and choice of selectors, while all prize-winners are selected by non-members of the committee.

The Society enjoys the support of the Arts Council, the County Council and the staff of the Usher Gallery. Again, Ken Lee feels it is important that the County's major gallery realises that the LAS provides 'The People's Show' – the artists of Lincolnshire on view to their county in their own gallery. With the coming of the new Museum adjacent to the Usher, and a new name – The Collection – covering both buildings, it is crucial that a Society with such a distinguished history and reputation should continue to find its home there.

Conclusion

In 1951 the Echo reviewer could write that the Lincolnshire Artists' Society was 'building a solid and a good tradition that might well be a 'Lincoln School' on the model of older schools like Norwich, Glasgow or St. Ives. Today in 2006 that building is surely complete. The Society had nurtured and produced the Lincoln School of Artists, and the time has come to talk about it and celebrate it.

From the start, the Society's founders were intent on receiving the kind of criticism that would enable their work to develop. This has never been a complacent or self-congratulatory Society. For a century, art critics and Royal Academicians have elevated it to a leading position, repeatedly singling out the work of Rollett, Worrall, Bartl, the Brannans, Oyler, Nadin, and Doitch. In their day, such artists as Boden, Coop, Pilcher and Garland achieved at least local fame. A great landscape tradition has evolved and continues to grow, while those who work in multi-media and favour an entirely abstract mode have found a Society eager for more and at ease with all forms of expression.

The Society is a great survivor. Innately conservative, as most societies are, it has welcomed those who did things differently and created waves. It has renewed itself through two World Wars, severe economic recession in Lincolnshire, and several alarming haemorrhages of Membership numbers. Its relationship with the Usher Gallery has been crucial and symbiotic, and its future will depend on the evolution of new relationships with its host.

Thanks to the LAS, the great artists of Lincolnshire's past do not have the final say. 50 years ago, Lincolnshire was still seen through the filter of Peter de Wint's elegiac paintings. Today we can see it through the eyes of Keith Roper.

Again, in my imagination, I take a summer's evening walk around old Lincoln, past the Usher, up the Greestone Stairs where Judith Oyler and Mary Dudding once lived, along the South side of the cathedral, past the Logsdail family home opposite the west front, then on past Tony Bartl's old studio and the Sam Scorer Gallery opposite, and finally down Gibraltar Hill. The evening sun transforms Lincoln, spread out to infinity below, and watching it all are Tony and Sheila Bartl and Sam Scorer. We chat about art, life and the local gossip. I don't remember the details, but as I take my leave, I feel that art matters…a lot. And it is clear that the Lincolnshire Artists' Society feels the same way.

Appendices

Appendix A

PRESIDENTS OF THE SOCIETY

W. T. Warrener	1930-34	Lord Brownlow	1979-82
No President1934-43		F. T. Baker	1983-93
Sir Hickman Bacon	1943-45	Peter Brannan	1993-94
Viscount Lord Crookshank	1945-61	Geoffrey Wilson	1996
The Earl Of Ancaster	1961-77	Peter Moss	1997-
The Hon. Edward Cust	1978		

Appendix B

CHAIRMEN OF THE SOCIETY

W. T. Warrener	1909-30	Gill Nadin	1976-77
T. G. Storey	1930-34	Audsley Power	1978-79
G. Boden	1934-35	M. Marschner	1980-81
C. C. Pilcher	1935-43	G. Wilson	1982-83
Austin Garland	1944-45	Gill Nadin	1984-85
G. Boden	1945-47	Dick Coon	1986-87
Kathleen Tyson	1947-50	S. Barrell	1988-89
S. Bullock	1950-51	Noel Black	1990-91
J. Marchbank Salmon	1952-53	Roy Perry	1992-93
P. G. Hodgkinson	1954-55	Keith Roper	1994-95
G. Farrow	1956-57	D. Paton	1996-97
Judith Oyler	1958-59	Gill Ross-Kelsey	1998-99
S. F. Barrell	1960-61	Fenella Stoner	2000-01
J. Grimble	1962-63	Cilla Chapman	2002-04
R. R. Alexander	1964-65	Carol Butler	2005
M. Brough	1965-67		
S. F. Barrell	1968-69		
Iona Cartwright	1970-71		
G. Wilson	1972-73		
R. W. Clark	1974-75		

Note: the dates show the actual calendar years when the office was held. With the AGM occurring late in the year until recently, new Chairmen took over in November and each served for two years, from 1944 to 2002, when it was decided they would serve in office for three years.

Appendix C

HONORARY SECRETARIES AND TREASURERS

SECRETARIES		TREASURERS	
Elsie Ruston	1906-09	Miss I. Hutton	1907-10
Mrs. R. Mason	1909-12	Mrs. H. Mence	1910-12
Mrs. H. Mence	1912-14	Mrs. R Mason	1912-19
FIRST WORLD WAR			
Miss R. Richardson	1919-21	Mrs. Gregorie	1919-22
Miss Nora Wright	1921	Mrs. Mason	1921-22
Mrs. Mason	1921-22	Miss Yeomans	1923-26
Austin Garland	1922-43	Austin Garland	1926-43
Francis Cooper	1943-60	Francis Cooper	1943-60
Kenneth Gribble	1960-67	Tom Baker	1961-70
John Foster	1967		
Tom Baker	1968-69		
Peter Williams	1970-75	Peter Williams	1970-79
David Morris	1975-76		
Bernard Brewer	1976-84	Charles Speed	1980-95
Joe Smedley	1984-87		
Janet Minty	1988		
Rosemary Lowery	1989-94	Micheal Logan	1995-97
David Morris	1995-99	John Maddison	1997-
Frank Marston	1999-		

Note: The dates given may not indicate the exact length of service, but indicate entire or almost entire years of service.

Appendix D

GUEST OPENER CRITICS OF THE ANNUAL EXHIBITIONS

1906	A. G. Webster	1950	Eric Newton	1979	Carel Weight
1907	George Clausen	1951	Robert Melville	1980	Bernard Dunstan
1908	H. Morley Fletcher	1952	Patrick Ferguson-Millard	1981	Roger De Grey
1909	A. Hartrick	1953	Barnett Freedman	1982	William Bowyer
1910	W. T. Warrener	1954	Edward Swann	1983	Ken Howard
1911	F. Cayley-Robinson	1955	Jack Merriott	1984	Stanislaw Frenkiel
1912	A. Jamieson	1956	Sir Albert Richardson	1985	William Varley
1913	A. Jamieson	1957	Edward Swann	1986	Alan Humberston
1914-19	No Exhibitions	1958	R. O. Dunlop	1987	Anthony Eyton
1920	John Wheatley	1959	Leonard Richmond	1988	Philip Race
1921	'MR Hatton'	1960	J. Marchbank Salmon	1989	Geoffrey Wilson
1922-4	No Names Recorded	1961	Colin Dudley	1990	Ton Baker
1925	No Critic Invited	1962	Harold Shelton	1991	Rigby Graham
1926	Fred Elwell	1963	No Critic	1992	Richard Bawden
1927	W. C. Penn	1964	A. Saunders	1993	Chris Sharp
1928-9	No Names Recorded	1965	Kenneth Long	1994	Peter Moss
1930	Gilbert Spencer	1966	Peter Lewis	1995	David Willetts
1931-35	No Names Recorded	1967	David Carr-Smith	1996	Peter Williams
1936	Norman Wilkinson	1968	John Aldridge	1997	Sam Scorer
1937	Not Known	1969	Edward Bawden	1998	Ken Howard
1938	C. C. Pilcher & A Garland	1970	Peter Williams	1999	Ben Levene
1939	Not Known	1971	Michael Gough	2000	John Howard
1940-43	Criticisms Suspended	1972	Not Recorded	2001	Julie Alsop
1944	Anna Airy	1973	No Critic	2002	Peter Moss
1945	Francis Hodge	1974	Peter Todd (?)	2003	Martin Postle
1946	Adrian Hill	1975	David Ainley	2004	David Paton
1947	Hesketh Hubbard	1976	Clifford Ellis	2005	Jo Volley
1948	R. Kirkland-Jamieson	1977	Ian Simpson		
1949	T. G. Dugdale	1978	Not Recorded		

Appendix E
LIST OF ORIGINAL MEMBERS

1906 Miss A. Aikenhead
St. Martin's Vicarage, Lincoln

1906 Mrs. Amcotts
Kettlethorpe Hall, Newark

1906 Mrs. Anderson
Frampton Hall, Boston

1906 Miss Anderson
Frampton Hall, Boston

1907 Miss Bergne-Coupland
Skellingthorpe Hall, Lincoln

1906 Mrs. Bergne-Coupland
South Clifton, Newark

1906 Miss Bland
Cheyne Walk, Chelsea

1907 Miss Bourne
Dunston Vicarage, Lincoln

1906 Mr. C. Brook
Pottergate, Lincoln

1906 Miss Leila Burton
Greestone House, Lincoln

1906 Lady Cholmeley
Normanby-by-Spital

1906 Mrs. Cracroft
Hackthorn Hall, Lincoln

1907 Miss O. Craster
Denton Rectory, Grantham

1906 Miss Dering Curtois
The Studio, Washingborough

1907 Miss Dalbiac
Radlett, Hertfordshire

1906 Mrs. Portman Dalton
Fillingham Castle, Lincoln

1906 Miss Denny
Stairhead, Lincoln

1906 Mrs. Duncombe-Anderson
Lea Hall, Gainsborough

1906 Miss Duigan
Lindum Holme, Bedford

1906 Mrs Gregorie
Burghersh Chantry, Lincoln

1906 Rev. Canon Harvey
Navenby Rectory

1906 Mrs. Walter Heape
Southwold, Suffolk

1906 Mrs. M. Hogarth
c/o The Times Book Club,
Oxford Street, London

1906 Miss I. Hutton
Vicars Court, Lincoln

1906 Miss M. D. Jeudwine
Harlaxton Rectory, Grantham

1906 Miss M. Kaye
Riseholme Rectory, Lincoln

1906 Miss J. Kennedy
James Street, Lincoln

1906 Mrs. King
The Manse, Bracebridge
Heath, Lincoln

1906 Miss R. M. H. Kinnear
The Red House, Nettleham

1906 Miss E. Leslie Melville
Welbourne Rectory, Lincoln

1906 Miss Mary Long
Swinderby Rectory, Lincoln

1906 Mrs. Macleod
11 Harley Street, London

1906 Miss Marriott
Governor's House, Lincoln

1906 Mrs. R. Mason
13 Drury Lane, Lincoln

1906 Miss Matthew
Lindum Terrace, Lincoln

1906 The Lady Eveline Maude
Thorney Hall, Newark

1906 Miss Sutton Nelthorpe
Scawby Hall, Brigg

1907 Mrs. E. Nevile
Skellingthorpe Manor, Lincoln

1906 Miss A. A. Pelham
Billesdon Coplow, Leicester

1906 Miss Piper
The Training College, Lincoln

1906 Miss F. Rawnsley
8 Norham Gardens, Oxford

1906 Miss Iris Reeve
21 Oxford Square, London

1906 Miss L. Richardson
Cold Bath House, Lincoln

1906 Major General Richardson
Halton House, Spilsby

1906 Miss E. Ruston
Monks Manor, Lincoln

1906 Miss Sedgwick
Grantham House, Grantham

1906 Hon. Ethel St. Leger
Pottergate, Lincoln

1906 Miss Nesta Stephenson
All Saint Vicarage, Tooting
Graveney

1907 Mrs. Hamilton Thompson
Exchequer Gate Lodge,
Lincoln

1906 Mr. W. T. Warrener
St. Margaret's Lodge, Lincoln

1907 Miss Wickham
The Deanery, Lincoln

1906 Miss E. Wilson
16 Watergate, Grantham

1906 Edith, Countess of
Winchelsea
Haverholme Priory, Sleaford

1906 Mrs. Young
Manor House, Metheringham

Appendix F

COMMITTEE 2005-2006

Peter Moss	President
Carol Butler	Chairman
Frank W. Marston	General Secretary
Jenny Hammerton	Deputy Chairman
Richard Hatfield	Hon. Exhibition Secretary
Margaret J. N. Dean	Hon. Membership Secretary
Hilary Brown	Publicity
Jackie Lee	Minutes Secretary

Appendix G

ELECTED MEMBERS OF THE COMMITTEE

Max Marschner
Janice Kok
Derek Roberts
Jenny Ellicott
Jeremy Webster

Appendix H

VICE PRESIDENTS

Lady Monson
David Morris
David Paton
Gillian M. Ross-Kelsey

Appendix I

LIST OF CURRENT MEMBERS

Margaret Addison
R. J. Armstrong
R. J. Bailey
Sheila Bartl
Gillian Beale
John Bearpark
Bea Bendelow
Brian Bicknall
K. M. Birch
S. L. Blatherwick
P. Bowman
Gillian Boyle
Rosie Bradshaw
Carol Bratley
T. E. J. Brooker
Hilary P. Brown
Peter Burgess
D. V. Burke
Carol Butler
Michael Caine
Jennifer Caine
John Callard
Barry Carter
Cilla Chapman
Terry Clarke
Mimi Claughton
Maurice A. Cole
Vivian Colley
Edith Cook
Dick Coon
R. A. Corcoran
Lynne Corcoran
R. S. Critchlow
Arthur Cross
Gail Das
Dianne J. Davies

M. J. N. Dean
Gail Deptford
W. J. Dixon
Bruce Duncan
Roy Ealden
Nick Ellerby
Jenny Ellicott
C. A. Emsley
Ann Everitt
Mary Fitzpayne
Jaqueline A. Gill
Janice Glew
Sarah L. Godfrey
Elizabeth Graydon
S. E. Hallam
Jenny Hammerton
J. A. Hancock
Shirley Harrell
Richard Harrison
Richard Hatfield
Denise Hawthorne
Neil Helyard
A. I. Hollingworth
D. Hollinshead
J. B. Horner
Vic Hotson
Pamela D. Hughes
Charlie Ip
Susan Jackson
Jilly Jenkins
Peter Johnston
Geraldine Jones
Janice M. Kok
K. Lee
Jacky Lee
G. P. J. Lewinton

J. C. Lincoln
Joan Lodge
M. A. Logan
A. Ludlam
Robert Machan
John Maddison
M. Marschner
Jill Marschner
Frank Marston
Ashi Marwaha
Caroline Mattaei
Rosemary Meijzner
Janet Minty
Hon M Monson
Peter Montgomery
N. D. Morris
Avril Morris
David Morris
Peter Moss
G. Nicholl
S. Parkinson
Jean Parsons
Brian Parsons
David Paton
Anthony Payne
David Alan
Annabel Pounder
Fiona Procter
Alexis Rago
Norah Ranshaw
Brian Raper
Brian Raynor
Derek Roberts
Keith Roper
Gillian M. Ross Kelsey
Jean Rowan

Dawn Rudderham-
Thornhill
Nigel Rutter
S. M. Sareen
J. Sargeant
Janet Schooley
Tracey Scott
Ralph Scott
P. R. Sheridan
Frederick A. Smith
Geoffrey E. Smith
Joyce Snowden
Charles Speed
Terence S. Stephens
L. Stoneham
F. Stoner
Jackie Strange
M. J. Taylor
Mo Teeuw
Michael Thacker
Letitia Thompson
Dorothy Trizis-Thorne
Dennis Valentine
Kevin Wallhead
Ian Watson
Jeremy Webster
Marjorie Wheeldon
Janet Whittle
Geoffrey Wilson
Alison Wilson
Elvira Witney
Keith Woodcock
J. M. Woods